THIRTY AUSTRALIAN POETS

THIRTY AUST- RALIAN POETS

EDITED BY FELICITY PLUNKETT

First published 2011 by University of Queensland Press
PO Box 6042, St Lucia, Queensland 4067 Australia

www.uqp.com.au

Cover design by Design by Committee
Typeset in 10.5/13 Adobe Garamond by Post Pre-press group, Brisbane
Printed in Australia by McPherson's Printing Group

This project has been assisted by
the Commonwealth Government through
the Australia Council, its arts funding
and advisory body.

National Library of Australia cataloguing-in-publication data
is available at http://catalogue.nla.gov.au

Thirty Australian poets / edited by Felicity Plunkett
ISBN: 9780702239144 (pbk)
              9780702247613 (pdf)

University of Queensland Press uses papers that are natural, renewable and recyclable products
made from wood grown in sustainable forests. The logging and manufacturing processes conform
to the environmental regulations of the country of origin.

CONTENTS

PREFACE

Emily Ballou's eponymous lizard, which sees its first page publication here, had an earlier airing. Chalked on a wall in Beirut, the poem found its first readers. At about the same time, two-year-old Jasper Alizadeh was boarding a plane from Dubai to Melbourne. 'Marco Polo', by his father Ali Alizadeh, is addressed to a child, Marco, inspired by Jasper. The poem's speaker faces the questions of an older version of his child to explain his parents' literal and figurative mobility; the question of 'why/we travel'.

In and through the poems in this collection we travel. From Bronwyn Lea's flooded Brisbane to Libby Hart's lone figure in Annaghmakerrig; from Danijela Kambaskovic-Sawer's migrant woman on an Australian bus thinking of Kundera to Ali Alizadeh's bus load of schoolchildren in Tehran thinking about Michael Jackson and into the quiet rooms where the poetic imagination moves, this collection gathers the energies of its generation.

Gathering energies, however, is perhaps sounder rhetorically than it is practically. A cluster of metaphors recurs in the description of Australian poetry, imagining its phases in the language of waves, generations and botany. John Tranter, interviewed in *Salt* in 1991, talks about the 'Generation of '68' . . . and his 'half serious theory that there are waves of new poetry in Australia', bringing together waves and generations in his discussion:

It was a wonderful time to be a writer, and the cultural shifts were even more exiting. Australia turned from being a closed-off, authoritarian, rather British village at the bottom of the planet to a much more open, cosmopolitan, adventurous society, fully at home in the modern world. The change went very deep into the structure of the society. And of course there were just as many interesting older poets around too, in those days; it wasn't just young people. The arguments, the conflict, the dialogue – these were all important in opening up the field of writing to more varied forms and different sources of energy.

In 2000, Michael Brennan and Peter Minter drew on the botanical in naming their collection of thirty contemporary Australian poets – a number of whom, including Brennan himself, are included here – in their anthology *Calyx* (Paperbark Press, 2000). 'Calyx' brilliantly collects connotations of the anatomical, the cerebral and the mythological. Brennan and Minter are mindful that anthologising 'can only ever be the result of partial, processual visions'.

The anthology, though, cannot entirely resist the taxonomical. In this case, the process of exploration takes the idea of the Generation of '68 and explores the work of thirty poets born in 1968 and beyond who have produced at least one book, as a practical way of making a start. As Tranter notes, though, not all emerging poets are young. A number of important emerging poets are slightly older than this: Nathan Shepherdson, David Musgrave and Kim Cheng Boey spring to mind. Others on the brink of publishing a first collection are among the poets whose work I await with anticipation – here I think of Fiona Wright and Eileen Chong, for instance. Then there are poets more or less connected with the Generation of '68 whose work continues to burgeon: Tranter, Pam Brown, Geoff Page. Conceits and catalogues with their necessary provisionality can, though, do the work of gathering and highlighting.

This anthology is a collaborative one, dependent on the generosity of poets themselves as well as the work of their publishers and editors. Poets' willingness for me to read work-in-progress and unpublished manuscripts has enabled us to publish new work alongside work that has already been acclaimed and awarded. UQP's tradition of publishing Australian poetry relies on the vision of its publishers. Madonna Duffy and John Hunter have both welcomed the idea of this anthology and supported its progress. And my colleagues at UQP have been crucial to the realisation of its vision: Kristy Bushnell, Tim McGuire and Michelle Law and especially the indefatigable and imaginative Rebecca Roberts. Ali Alizadeh and John Turner have been generous interlocutors, and Callan Moroney's help has been vital. It is a privilege to include an introduction by David McCooey, whose stellar academic career should not obscure his talents as a poet. And John Tranter, whose words here enrich the collection, and who has published, edited and mentored many of this generation, is, in many ways, an inspiration.

Felicity Plunkett

INTRODUCTION

How to begin? Poets deal with this problem routinely. A poem is always a new beginning, a way of struggling with long-standing questions such as 'What is a poem?' and 'Who is my audience?' Every new poem answers the question, 'How can I start again?'

This anthology of work by thirty Australian poets begins with the editorial decision to focus on poets born since 1968, gathering writers who have generally published one or two full-length collections and established themselves within the last decade. This anthology doesn't present a 'group' or a 'movement', but rather a way of seeing a particular demographic of poets. This demography is diverse, ranging from poets with non-Anglophone backgrounds, such as Ali Alizadeh and Danijela Kambaskovic-Sawers, to expatriate poets, such as Emma Jones and Louis Armand, to the Indigenous poet Samuel Wagan Watson. Most notably, it illustrates the central role of women in contemporary Australian poetry. Of the thirty poets represented here, eighteen are women, surely an unprecedented (and belated) statistic in Australian poetry anthologies.

Felicity Plunkett's decision to concentrate on poets born after 1968 is both a filtering device and an elegant gesture towards the 'Generation of '68', that older group of poets who have dominated recent histories of Australian poetry. The Generation of '68 – the name invokes the international spirit of revolution that marked 1968 – designates a moment of Australian cultural revolution at the beginning of the 1970s when a group of poets sought to 'modernise' Australian poetry. It was a time marked by factionalism and polemic.

The poets in this anthology are, chronologically, post-68ers. But what does this mean in poetic terms? How has the most recent 'generation' of poets responded to the current condition of poetry? How has the 'revolution' of the 1970s played out into the new millennium? Is the current discussion (largely confined to the blog-osphere) about a supposed turn towards 'traditional' lyric poetry, away from avant-gardist practices, borne out in the poetry?

Recent commentary on Australian poetry – in reviews, essays, and blogs – often begins with a complaint about poetry's small audience and the apparently dwindling attention it receives from publishers and the media. But regardless of problems of audience and distribution, there is ample evidence that Australian poetry is exceptionally healthy in terms of production. Much superb Australian poetry has been published in recent years, and there has been an extraordinary flowering of strong debut collections, many by poets represented here. This anthology, then, appears at a time when Australian poetry is undergoing a powerful – if somewhat paradoxical – revitalisation.

The poetry collected here represents the complex ways in which such revitalisation is occurring, ways that make sharp distinctions between 'traditional' lyric and avant-garde poetics difficult to maintain. The poets collected here are diverse not only in terms of background, but also style. Their work ranges from the complex ambiguities of Armand and Kate Fagan, to Lisa Gorton's exact lyricism, Alizadeh's powerful mix of allegory and realism, and Emma Jones's inventive meditations on the nature of representation. Tonally, poems range from the almost-ecstatic 'Colorado River Prayer' by Kate Middleton to the shocking bluntness (and humour) of Maria Takolander's sequence on pregnancy, 'Unborn'. This latter poem in turn offers an interesting contrast to Esther Ottaway's riddling poem on being pregnant, 'Dimension and Light'. Michelle Cahill writes poetry that is simultaneously lush and unsentimental, while Justin Clemens's baroque-like poems are tonally ambiguous, resolutely refusing to offer clear horizons of expectation for their readers.

Such a refusal adverts to a powerful feature of the poetry in this collection: it does not apologise for itself. This poetry takes risks, including the risk of 'difficulty'. One might argue that such difficulty is related to another major feature of this anthology's demographic. If the Generation of '68 was the first generation of poets to generally have access to tertiary education, the poets here are the first generation to generally have PhDs. Two thirds of the poets represented here have, or are working towards, higher degrees. This is an extraordinary situation and one that might be seen, in Australia, as demanding apology.

But apologising for this generation – or writing it off – as 'academic' would be to profoundly misunderstand these poets. However informed their work is by academic knowledge (not to mention the academic virtues of intellectual inquiry, openness, and independence), these poets are profoundly engaged with poetic problems, and with the question 'How to begin?' As a consequence, their work shows a profound knowledge of poetic precedence, that source of any poetic beginning. A number of poems employ ancient forms such as the catalogue and the dialogue. Others revise earlier poetry. LK Holt and Kambaskovic-Sawers, for instance, both revisit *The Odyssey* with an attention to gender, while David Prater rewrites Bernard O'Dowd's 'Australia' as 'Oz'. Jaya Savige's 'La Quercia Del Tasso' thematises poetic precedence, with the poem's speaker leaning against the oak tree associated with the sixteenth-century Italian epic poet Tasso (who suffered from mental illness and died shortly before being made poet laureate). This poem on poetic precedents, appropriately enough, has its own precedent: Peter Porter's 'Tasso's Oak'. Others here respond more generally to cultural history, as seen in Emily Ballou's poems on Charles Darwin. Elsewhere we find references to *The Kalevala* (the 'national epic' of Finland), Michael Jackson's *Thriller*, and the poems of Emily Dickinson.

Does such a wide (one might say 'postmodern') intertextuality make this poetry 'obscure'? I would argue that it doesn't. In the

Google age nothing is obscure, at least at the level of reference. Anyone reading this book with access to the internet can easily find out who Sun Ra was, what Kundera wrote, or who wrote a forty-part motet. Intertextuality, then, need no longer be seen as an index either of obscurity or cultural elitism. A more open, and pluralist, response to such writing is to see these poets as intensely receptive to the multiple histories, subjectivities, and cultures available to them.

Such openness could be seen as running counter to the 'little-Australia' mentality that marked John Howard's prime ministership and the years since (that is, the years these poets have been most active). Such a mentality is most evident in Australian attitudes to asylum seekers, but it is also discernable in political debate about immigration generally. In such a context, this anthology is notably cosmopolitan in scope, bringing together immigrant poets, expatriate poets, and poetry originally published by international publishers. Perhaps even more notably, there is a profound 'worldliness' to this collection that puts the designation 'Australian' under numerous creative tensions.

Part of this worldliness is no doubt a response to the violent ways that the national and the global have intersected in the last decade, as the references to the so-called War on Terror in poems by Joel Deane and John Mateer suggest. The work in this anthology, however, is not simplistically political, nor is it primarily concerned with the worldliness of cultural reference. The rich complexities of the quotidian, momentary experience, and emotion – especially as those things are continuous with their cultural representations – are all concerns central to this collection, as seen in the haunting poems by Sarah Holland-Batt, Bronwyn Lea, and Cameron Lowe.

Out of this concern with the everyday we see this collection also strongly concerned with human relationships. This concern is especially notable, though not exclusively so, in the poetry by women. As Gorton's acerbic 'The Affair' illustrates, it is not a sentimental concern, even as it accommodates itself to the age-old poetic theme of love. In Libby Hart's hands, the theme of love takes on an elegiac note, whereby lone figures inhabit the ghost-filled landscape of Ireland, which takes us back to this anthology's 'worldliness'.

The poetry collected here is as entertaining as it is challenging. It engages the reader intellectually and sensually, offering the resistance necessary for the play of interpretation. One of the most entertaining features of this collection is its arrangement. While the poets are arranged in neutral alphabetical order, Felicity Plunkett (a superb poet herself) has chosen the poems so that the collection reads like a 'book', with artfully repeating motifs and themes. Birds, night, water, and mouths appear repeatedly (the last three of which all appear in Wagan Watson's 'Revolver'). Ancient Egyptians appear three times, while cats, those Egyptian deities, feature in numerous poems. Most powerfully, the moon is the source of seemingly endless metaphorical invention. That the moon is such a hackneyed poetic image, and that it is so powerfully rendered here, is further evidence of Australian poetry's strength.

Having begun, how does one end? It would be foolish to try to find a single term (such as 'neo-romantic' or 'minimalist') with which to categorise these poets. The poets represented here are both profoundly various and powerfully related. Often stylistically rich, almost baroque, they can also engage in plain talking. If these poets are not happy with the state of poetry in public culture, they are nevertheless not drawn (unlike their predecessors) into making wild claims about their art. At home in the pluralist, ironic world of the postmodern, they also engage in the ancient poetic project of renewal. As Felicity Plunkett's collection demonstrates, there is – thankfully – no end to making new poems that allow us to see our lives, and history, and the moon in new ways.

David McCooey

ALI

ALIZADEH

LISTENING TO MICHAEL JACKSON IN TEHRAN

after Azar Nafisi

Smuggled across the fierce chasm
between us and the US, and then

hidden, stuffed between Farsi
and Science textbooks in my school

bag, the illegal and sacrilegious
cassette-tape of *Thriller*, ready for

revelation to the sheepish, ignorant
kids on the bus to my primary school

in war-stricken Tehran. My plan:
to expose the forbidden thing, exhibit

my courage, rebelliousness, etc. Autumn
of '83, desperate for attention/approval

from the other kids. My copy of
dangerous Western 'art' would

unsettle the boring, Islamic world
of my classmates – and elevate my

cowardly, chubby, unpopular
self. I whispered to the kid next to me

if he had ever heard of 'Billie Jean'
and 'Beat It'; if he knew anything at all

about *the number one famous
star* of our wicked enemy. "I love

Thriller! Aren't the zombies so scary
in the music video! They're so ugly!" His

boisterous words echoed. The bus
vibrated with the singer's name. Another

shouted he had a *Thriller* poster, and
another, a 'Billie Jean' T-shirt, a gift from

Turkey. Silenced, robbed of my planned
stardom, I sank in my seat; later threw out my

Thriller tape, the fetish of Great Satan's
useless, ubiquitous popular culture.

EXILE AND ENTROPY

I sink in the leather of my chair
a donkey, can't bother with braying

in a bog. Village animal in the marsh,
an image to denote dislocation: removed

from Tehran's clamorous scenes
of coups, rallies and revolutions

to an island. Here rain makes the headlines
and 'history,' a post-script to 'sport'. Not

only boredom but the erasure
of mother tongue – the proclivity for

voicing a rope to clench
and crawl out of the swamp. Why

bother getting to my feet if beyond this
lies nothing but monumental contempt

in the eyes of neighbours and the spectre
in the mirror? Hope, penitence,

nostalgia can't soften or graze the hardness
of their gaze. Stuck in mire

cloistered by a thicket of stony reeds
I'm here to 'start anew'. In Tehran

I could at least explode and screech. Now
the thermodynamics of my body

amass, contort. How to convert them
to something kinetic? In any case, entropy

means decline or at least chronic
disorganisation. To be sure, desire

boils emotions in my mind's engine
but body doesn't move. It wanes

in the swamp's mud, here
behind this desk, my muscles sag

submerged in exile, thoughts simmer.

MARCO POLO

Maybe it's the natural
extension of immigration. Maybe

it's the awesome travel
bugs, making my wife's feet

uncommonly itchy. I'm not
surprised, at any rate, to hear

the paediatrician's nickname
for our son. 'Marco Polo' suits

his – in utero – trajectory
along the Silk Road, from

Kublai Khan's Forbidden City
to the snow-covered stones of a caravanserai

in central Turkey. Not to mention
the Australian interregnum

where ultrasound scans
revealed his sex. But our Marco

probably won't pen a *Travels*
as he won't know the other

of unending expedition, say,
cherished waterways of Venice, in short

a concrete home. Are we monstrous
parents? Why have we conceived

and delivered a life into the world
in transition? If held to account

by a solicitous young man
with my eyes (and my wife's better

eyebrows) one day, accused
of depriving him of his deserved

comforts of sedentary genesis
(motherland, mother tongue

two ebullient grandmothers, etc)
I can only offer an image: removing

picture frames, tribal ornaments
from the hooks; clearing the drawers

of wrinkled notepads with withered ideas
and perforated socks; tearing

the hooks off the walls. And then
the bright outline of the picture frames

vacated on the otherwise drab
dust-darkened surface of the wall. It's this

record of the passage of time
the contrast between the original

preserved shade and colour
and the rest (ditto our lives) dog-eared

by mould, sunlight, scratches
of nature and accidents. It's this

visible discrepancy between
what we were and what we've become,

the possibility to uncover
and see it. The nomads treasure

wisdom: the reality of ageing
towards death. You see, Marco

– I'll tell him – if we can see
death looming, like a dark island

on the navigator's horizon
then we won't be shocked when

time's run out. This means
a life without our primal fear. That's why

we travel.

I, THE MONSTER

I, the monster
you, the angel

are humans?
My fangs are plastic,

your wings paper;
human-made to signify

un-humanity. Such
poetry this

deformation of
reality. No, I don't

mean truth, the source
of this elaborate

fairytale. Let the gods
play at that

as Euripides might say
'from their ethereal thrones'.

Mine is more like
a dilapidated toilet-seat

all too earthly
for the theatrics of divinity.

That makes me
monstrous? Abject?

Still too polite to say
'Can I borrow thy whitish wing

to wipe my arse?'
I play my part

in the drama of The Battle.
Such an actor

I look so defeated
toppled by your gleaming

Archangel Michael.
There. The crowds cheer

and overcome
their humanity.

Backstage I help you
slash your heavenly wrists

upon my blunted horns.
I know you'll win this war

too. I'm the archetypal
loser. At your funeral

the crowds howl louder than ever.
I'm all too indifferent

all too monstrous
to hold back my tears.

RUMI

I escaped from the city
barefooted. I escaped from the fires

naked, except for the bag
of ancient books

slung over my back.
I ran into the desert. The horsemen

chased. Their torches
had coloured the tenements.

I ran for months. Finally
on a glorious night

I stopped. The raiders had given up
on me. I was alone

with the moon and the sand-dunes.
I looked down at my feet.

They were skinned.
I looked at my trace: red footprints

dark on the glowing plain.
I thought about my tribe

butchered as sacrificial beasts.
I remembered their smiles

before the flames. On the holy night
I knelt before the moon

and wept. In the desert
tears are elixir. From their pool

a fountain bubbled. I cleaned my scars
in the water. The books

weighed on my body. I took them out
and one by one

dipped them into the spring.
All knowledge, all art, and all history

drowned before my eyes. Freed
from the clutch of paper

words' ink dissolved in the lake.
I then drank. I was saved.

LOUIS

ARMAND

PATRICK WHITE AS A HEADLAND

Something vast is being suggested,
shapes barely visible in the
pre-dawn – a faint line of smoke
from a chimney – or a headland
                    bearing down at the sea
                    like an ego, jutting into it,
describes the laborious theosis
of a body at the end of a
grappling hook – *to bleed if necessary*
to ascend – and the seasurge beating at the shore,
                    thick turbulent
yellow water – and the dark crab-eyes
looking into it, long after
                    there was anything left to see

UTZON

*I got much more from some charts of the sea I obtained in
Copenhagen – from these I could measure the distances and
form a judgment of heights*

Jørn Utzon

1. Concrete primal naked forms / the anti-
constructs of

cranes / stooping
low
over the quays

theme and
variation

the harbour's in-
violate curve
describing

simultaneous contrast / in sections of
scaffolded light

2. . . . . c.1970 *le repos
du modèle* (vivisection of
the nude, industrial

sub-
cutaneous geometries
proliferate

towards incompletion)
sur cette verge
terrestre

an immovable sphinx
absorbed
in its own enigma

3. "A sail surmounts the steep slope
of this
          white profile"
(lit from behind,
the incongruous body had to be
arranged *pictorially* –
investigation of depth
study of volumes, measures –
a radial (system) of convex
                    and cylindrical surfaces . . .)

4. Withdrawn beneath its shell – the sea
enormous and delicate
as a soprano – allegory of "words
that have no (other) past . . ."

Shaped along an axis of the in/visible –
its weight of hollow sentiment falling
in sculptured folds about the spectral
body (ciphered in fake notations of

perspective), or an eyelid caught mid-beat
and dark iris looking out through a haze
of rain on discoloured wave-forms
which nevertheless remain detached

from "natural history": emblematic of what,
there, barely remains / no longer remains

5. Against the sky its reflection becomes overcast:
ambivalence in lieu of the arduous labour,
or paradigm for representing death? Its veils
mockingly fatalistic, as the ever-arched backs
of endlessly repeating question marks.
Perceived at a distance this wave-motioned
ballet mécanique resembles a process
                              in differing stages of term-
ination – casting the delayed substance
in ratio to ephemerality – and always in retreat
from that impossible traverse, rigor mortic
in the too-literal gaze of conscientious on-lookers

SOMETHING LIKE THE WEATHER

(to John Forbes, et al.)

1. It begins and in spite of everything (sleeplessness,
fear of attack) is almost serene. Shooting speed
in a room behind the GPO, each letter
one more step in the direction of universal literacy.
Nobody needs poetry for this. Or do they?
Witness our little ceremonies, the nightwatchman's
redemptive vision, the hairdresser's assistant
like some hapless *Venus of Urbino* draped in her
sleek reclining chair. Tomorrow we may slip out
past the wire-conducting trees into the languages
of the news stands. Or sit alone, white serviette
folded into smaller and ever smaller epigrams.
You check the dials, the registers, the glass eyes.
Could anything have happened in the meantime?

2. "The visible in materialisation is not the material."
Old Quiros waiting to cross the road – then
the coffee arrives. You notice, how he stood there
deliberately, like a ruined observation post, framed
by the corner window at the station kiosk. All those
elapsed times, cut-out faces in green commuter busses.
First light. Floating through billboard retail scenes.
Quiros in his drunken boat paddling towards
Elizabeth Street. 8.00 a.m. and progressively the air
becomes rubberised and limp. Piecing together
an itinerary of what's left to come: this hour
meant for nothing more, having struck root in us,
stroked and shaped and misintended by it.
The same repeated hour, the same deliberation.

3. One of the ten plagues of Egypt made its way even
here. Slouching under the harbour on hollow legs,
to re-emerge, strangely intact, propped against
a bar in Harold Park holding forth on Michelet's
Historical Monuments. And this, as good or bad
as any other place to live and die in. Television
made the outside world invisible; poetry made it a
wreck. In each particular a ritual has been arranged –
the metrical progress of footfall up the stairs,
a closing door, a too insistent respiration. Things
there are hardly notions to impress upon. Asleep again
under the moon-broadening night, the sound of
police helicopters, the broken-bottled serenades and
street hustlers bidding dreams of wordless fornication.

4. Something to be filed away on the internal memex.
Nights of bondage fed on the wholly unreal, a city
dredged-up from barbarous pre-history, crime or
Wanderlust. You know the score, tapping out rhymes
on the shoulder of adversity, for the sake of a look
or as little as an admonition. The truth was never
believable, in any case. We have invented the worst
as best we can, always reflecting the contrary of intention.
Underfoot the banging becomes more and more hellish
and idiotic. (Why won't the dead finally shut up and
sleep?) The distance travelled is still not far enough.
The migraine purrs. Morning shouts in its familiar drawl.
A dry meniscus rings the eye, thickening over it, caul-
like. And how the dumb horrors laugh.

ROLAND ROBINSON'S GRENDEL
& DEATH IN CUSTODY

An unseen hand at work among the evidence. Grendel re-
shuffling the pages, strata, bone-shards and whatever else
remains, as indictment or disqualification. Our deletions
are accumulating, like Royal Commissions or radio talk-back.

Grendel and John Laws exchanging product placement
between early morning traffic reports. To start again
bending the square outline of a place in which nothing
escapes formulation, hanging cheap tinsel on everything.

Or a landscape with empty refrigerators, detention cells,
uselessly speaks the way of refuse or refusal.
Grendel in Redfern, breaking off TV aerials and clothesline
to make a bed. Grendel beckoning at the window,

all dark hints and bodily purpose. Knowing as well as you do
there's no such thing as accidental death in custody.

EMILY
BALLOU

THE PLUMS

in the bowl
on the round table
by the windows
were laid out for
his father.

That pyramid of dark plums
in the shallow Wedgwood bowl—
nearly black when ripe
ruby-lipped when not
oily, reflective, satin-skinned
piled on a plate in the sun—
infinitely pinchable, infinitely delicate, hot
when Charles touched them
when he inserted the tip of his smallest finger
into their dark navels
from which stems had long fallen.

If his father waited too long
to eat them, the plums
would wrinkle & weep
rubbed under thumbs.

At first Charles would pocket a few
pile them in the stores cupboard
or under the piano lid
& reap the glory when he found them
again, his father's missing fruit.

Then he began to flinch a bite of one, two
searching out the perfect plum.
He pulled the skin off them with his teeth
watched beads of blood pinprick the surface
ripped bits of peeling
around the pink sponge.
Old plums were soft & purple, not crisp.
New plums sour & crunched
too much, hard yellow pulp
inedible. He left them all
ruined by the river
the single bite he'd taken from each
like a torn smile.

IN THE OLD LIBRARY

Where John Milton
'The Lady of Christ's' & son of a scrivener once sat
composing his Latin oration:
Sportive Exercises on occasion do not stand in the way
of Philosophical Studies
after recovering from a first year
quarrel with his tutor over his assertive, unusurpable singularity
(which resulted in short suspension, not to mention
a good caning at the hands of the Master)
to become one of the more playful & popular fellows,
creating such cunning prolusions as the above as well as
       breaking out
into heroic couplets instead of the usual formal tongue
& leaving behind among the twine & leather-bound
book & tome-stacked shelves a lasting battle
of light & darkness, 'a little world' not yet spent
so two hundred years later
Charles Darwin, pale & Paleyfied, just twenty-one,
solemnly bent his head & read
his favourite poem.

PLUNGE

You thrust your head through a lid of water
open-eyed to the sting of salt
that takes some time to adjust to
then look around.
Your curls swim. Fish scatter.

Pink velvet starfish cling to the green
slopes of sub-aqueous rock pools, the diorama spill
of strange flowers, opening, shutting mouths
draw you deeper
past grey-eyed cuttlefish
the circular gills barely perceptible
feathered edges of constant motion among the waving
fronds of seaweed hair & the rise & pop of silver
domes of air.

Here a corrosive, rusted land
beneath land, a forgotten twin place
on Earth where Man
does not belong, where sea
divides head from body
so thoroughly it is exiled;
the floating flesh
so much whiter, more defenceless;
this total, plunging, breathless despair.

Terror makes you leap up
suddenly from the depths
& laugh to find you were dunked
head down in two feet of water.

Go now. Deeper. Into the blue swallow.
If you're lucky enough you'll catch
a fever of sting rays
soaring past the ship in sinuous series
the great, slate, rugose weights;
little bodies embedded in wings.

When you capture one
& flip over its flat white belly, on the sand,
a small false face appears:
the side-gazing eyes
the nose-holes of its snout, the slit
of mouth gills dimpled on either side
like a smile—
wide, distended, intelligent
underwater humanity
you slice with a knife.

Nights when the sea
& everything you touch
lights up green, pours over you
mass & massive

you will remember
Volta's batteries
which he called his electric fish
& which were puzzled out
from the anatomy
of stingrays.

SHE PLAYED

pianoforte for him
when his hands trembled
from dissecting
too many luminous creatures aquatic
eyes flinching like filaments.
Microscopic tremors.

She played with the yellow lamp
on her left
casting light softer than moth
wings over her skin.

The plaintive tapping
of her satin slipper
her slim foot rising & falling
filled & calmed him.

How much more immediate
were the effects of music on his mind, his spine.

All throughout tea
he'd waited for this time.

Sometimes he watched her fingers
climb the chords, as though many-legged,
ravelling & unravelling clues
like Hume's witty, infinite spider
spinning the world from its bowels.

Sometimes she played Bach
with a parlour-pervading sadness
her face otherwise rarely possessed

but mostly she played Mozart
though not by heart.

LIZARD'S FIRST LAW OF INERTIA

Lizard saw that rocks wanted to be at rest on the Earth
and that smoke wanted to be at rest in the sky
and the stars wanted to remain where they had been flung.
He thought that a body was in its natural state when it was still
and for his body to move in a straight line at a constant speed
no force but his own was needed to maintain the velocity.
Though wind helped occasionally with acceleration.
And the sun.

[From the world according to Lizard]

JUDITH

BISHOP

IT BEGINS WHERE YOU STAND

The *tap, tap* is nearly not a sound at all.
But when you hear it,
it makes the spring air about it hollow
and its own. It reaches to the dappled plane trees
along the dusty road, across to a yellow bike
parked against a pole.
                              And it begins
where you stand, below the window pane
of an old apartment, onto which
an orange beak—a female cardinal—graphs
for the dreamer in his bed
the resonance of frosted glass,
                                        against
the shifting speed of insects,
                                        multiplied
by the general, growing hunger of the season.
As the boy groans, the cardinal morse-
codes her intuition
that the wind, within the hour, will have turned
toward the east;
and spawned a tornado in its wake.

OPENINGS

I could say hello to things.
Theodore Roethke

i.
The hand's wave,
when it comes—
formal, yet never once the same,
awkward sometimes,
sometimes half-
withheld—
from the sunlight of the brain
makes a shadow of intent.

Something alights
in the meadow of vision.
Shimmering,
electric,
each datum's serene
in its dance of *arrival from the world*—
each met by the sprightly
pas-de-deux of the brain,
holiest union,
whose coda unfolds
in the body's
archipelagos of darkening
roads,
where the nerve
bulb flashes
and winks out.

ii.
Loveliness and horror pass through
the open gate.
Appear in the field,

and the widening ripples
begin, startled dancers
and audience beyond, all places in the brain
where the judgments
rise and shout.
How do you open
the gate to a birth?
How do you
open the door on a death?
Open, knowing what must
dart out like a cat;
open, knowing
how the rush will numb the fingers
to any further action,
and the mind
be transfixed before the scene.

iii.
Does the tree return her greeting
when a child says hello?
Something happens in the interval of love,
it must, for though the air
is unmoved, time opens and floats
like the seeds
of a dandelion clock.

Then call the tree
by its name:
like the unicorn,
it steps into your mind
and will remain.

iv.
She came to the door
one afternoon, she said,
Have you seen my brother,

we've been calling for a week,
my mother's
worried.
Our neighbour, who was friendly
and young,
kept unusual hours. His door
absorbed her knocking, *back,*
back, back, back, an
uncrossable field.
At last she said, I'll go
get the police.
A quiet hour passed.
Then we heard the door
opened, we heard
a woman weeping at the sight.

v.
Yellow leaves on black water,
weeping willow,
and farther, the tree entire mirrored
for a child too young to understand
the doubling
of a thing between image and is,
how the flapping duck scours off the duck afloat on water
as it rises
into all and only what it is, in air.
This is the time
when what does not exist, begins to.
Symbol and thing acquiesce in their merger,
one and the other
are met by the child
with equanimity, the willow
weeps and is greeted
both in water and in air.

ISSUANCE

And so I have become
this slow poem of mouths resisted—
paraphrasing my desire
from the stones of a river.

I might have held his body
for the thought alone that he
could not be owned,
or what it is to listen low—

but I rode my bones' panic
through the tail of fallen dusk.
I walked unlit into the hills of pine.

MICHAEL BRENNAN

LETTER HOME

I've tried not to think about him
for the last six months

but he creeps inside, angry at this
need for self-preservation.

Some days the Underground melts
into confusion. I've seen him

down there, a hundred times a day,
a practical joke gone too far.

There's no turning back
like Orpheus.

The olds figure he's up ahead,
rebuilding a Torana from spare parts,

grease and dirt under his nails.
I'm still waiting for the call

where I hear his voice again, its
subdued smile, the gentle monotone

rambling through design faults of
Ford motors without breath.

I doubt there's an after-life
other than the one we live here.

Today it rests in an image
already twenty years old:

David stripping down a chassis,
the orange flash of brake fluid

catching, his ear-to-ear grin
not even remotely like the dusk.

LETTER HOME

These are strange lands I barely understand.
We are walking in a park of manicured lawns.

The sky is a mosaic of syllables,
Parts of a puzzle.

The people here douse themselves in petrol
As though poetry mattered.

Some of the pieces are missing
And the old man tells me we have to make new some new ones.

He looks through me. It matters little if I am here.
In a corner of the park monks are burying elephants.

I found a word under my tongue
But swallowed it whole.

The lawn is a lesson in geometry, it imitates
The cast of the concrete walls,

I don't know if the grass is grey or the concrete grass.
None of it looks like the sky, least of all the sky.

Fashioned out of water, paths no one walks on
Lead into proximity.

The old man spits out tones that sit in pools on the water,
Half-oil, half-mercury, he tests them with one foot.

In the distance someone or something catches fire.
Perhaps it is the elephants coming into bloom.

THE OTHER

He has been drinking
in my father's coat
slowly filling it with laughter.
There are histories he tells
I am no longer sure I have lived
or simply dreamt stretched in
the long grass of past summers.

Sometimes he murmurs
in the dark, *We dream the real.*

Rising the other morning
it seemed he stole love from me,
returning its shadow. Little by little
I have surrendered everything
to him. There may be new love
in the morning but first
there must come the night.

Sleep arrives slowly,
carrying the face of a stranger.

LETTER HOME

I find him
by the path,
his stone shoulders
overgrown
with moss
and lichen,
his smiling face
erased completely
by centuries of
rain and wind.
I sit beside him
for the barest
moment, feet
heavy and close
to the earth, ground,
the day's heat cooled
and gathering, our bodies
whole again and unfamiliar,
returned from
the infinitesimal
fragments
we share.

REBIRTH

Yet another morning and I get a sense
the world has been given a second chance,
the first touch of warmth rising white
and fine from the hollows of night.

Breathe a sigh of relief, ponder the nebulous
ways that brought you to this rebirth
of circumstances beyond your control,
how you became movement and rest

between particular things, such as the residual coffee
on your mug's rim, not unlike scurf still clinging
shore, or layers of ancient weather systems drawn
up from some arctic ice shelf, and the miracle

that all of this has something to say to you
particularly, you there, in your freshly laundered
underwear rubbing sleep from your eyes,
so happily befuddled to find we are all far from

alone setting forth here, trundling about
the spaceship Earth, unsure of our destination.
Go out now, time-traveller, read your future,
on the rings of some ancient tree and consider

your prophecies carefully, between collecting
your dry cleaning and the morning papers,
between the cosmic small talk and chit-chat
the world and you are revolving elliptically about,

shifting into hints and premonitions of some
grander pattern, that you might see much later,
rising unscientifically, say, in the look of surprise
that surfaces on her face in a smile anciently encoded

in your shared DNA, when love first fell through you,
a look that to the curious and persistent might remind
each speck of us of the stardust from which
we are constantly and mindlessly evolving.

MICHELLE
CAHILL

TWO SOULS

My cat cries when I enter the garden, as
if I have aroused her from winter's dream
or as if she wants to sing to me, her name.

What do cats dream of, Lord Krishna?
A coconut shell of milk or a glittering fish?
Now her slender limbs complete their *asanas*.

Now her neck arches, her jaw, an elastic.
The sharp eye constricts, discerns wind
in the quivering grass from a grasshopper's

camouflage. But there's no mistaking Maya.
My cat rehearses the accurate lunge of her paw.
She cries as one compelled, hungry, yet not.

Perhaps my being here deserves an answer.
For weeks I too have watched her, how
she hunts. I've heard the moan of her catch

at dusk, which is your hour, Lord Krishna.
Then, no bird sings and only a cat with two souls
dreams of death, her stigma left on a lizard

or on a butterfly, whatever moves towards
the shadow of meaning. As I am born of fire
I burn, my Lord, but I sleep in your arms.

I am one Upanishad moon on fragrant nights.
By day I am the consort of oceans, rice fields,
pale and invisible to you as the sky's temple.

KISSING HAMLET

A sparrow falls by providence, and the evening sky
is smeared indigo. I won't repeat our darling word
dusk, since breaking old habits is a new promise.
Sometimes the heart locks, before it dangles, ready
for releasing. Something in the amorphous shape
the trees espouse at this time of day is a resistance
to anything particular or complex, as if a more subtle
variation were possible. A toning down of contrast
makes the hour we named for us a kind of yielding.
'We are something', you say, and I try to believe.
But even as I write, the sky's streaks fade, the burls
of cloud formations begin to disappear, obeying
Newton's third law that for every act in this universe
there is an equal and opposite one. Today I walked
the streets, observing what I've missed of late—
a white magnolia in full bloom with delicately scented
petals, chaste as Ophelia, among the topiary plants;
a house in ruins becoming some ugly new development.
And, of course, I thought of us—that hole we cut
in the stillness of evening, when the heart is disposed
to abandon the thought of never wanting this to stop.
The heart is mute but cries out in protest: *Be free,*
what are you afraid of? Advice I tested last night
at the Opera Bar. I kissed the princely lips of madness:
Hamlet himself, after the proscenium. Not yet drunk.
His eyes, untamed, a little lost, perhaps. I trembled
but he didn't seem to mind, and I was glad, recalling
a soliloquy which speaks of fate's occasion being fickle,
how the end is ever present, how *the readiness is all.*
The harbour slapped softly, in Luna Park the Ferris wheel
turned. At least every so often, it is good to tremble.
And somehow the moment cured me of the incomplete

metaphor of madness I had taken for myself. So moments
change us, the evening bleeds and bruises. Words come
to me as freely as a sparrow falls, unfastened by the sky.

I lay her under a camellia bush by the stone Buddha,
where a cherry blossom scattered its confetti karma,
where azaleas flourished and minah birds convened.
Her pelt had been tattooed by a powerline. Night fell.
I almost forgot her because I was exhausted,
because I couldn't sleep, bypassing all attendant
thought of mourning. Outside the brushwood
stirred with native ghostings: her kind, not the shape
of hunger but death's apprentice slipping through trees,
their wire fingers scuffed against sky. The mist paused,
as if it were autumn, the trees were bare tightropes.
By daylight there were catkins, magpies broke the dawn,
the sky pinned back its rain. Leaves were floating carp,
wisteria festooned desiccated gardens. I walked past lilies
with elephant ears swaying in the sun, a stop sign pulled
out from the ground by schoolboys. All this to slake me,
to dress my grief: these things with names to keep or to speak
as if articulation made of thought a substance.
Words, falling softly as feathers or pollen. How many words
might a woman discern? And what of a small marsupial
shocked by current, mid-climb, lit-up in free-fall?
What made me crush a blossom of wisteria to sprinkle
over the small, dead thing? Away I went to read the day's
diffuse paragraphs, to bluff my way through colouring-in,
a daughter's grammar. She ties toys with paperclip chains,
devices infinite to bind or to banish. Cars flew by,
a truck with a skip-bin, birds scavenged from the tarmac.
Up close, the possum smelt like rancid butter. I sat with
her and smoked, hearing nothing. No pity, no slight
for what I'd named her, *Sweet Shadow-Playing Funambulist*.
What was the harm? I might call her a crumpled stocking,
a ripple in the field, or a girl's dismembered evidence.

The swing tempts her back. Trucks pass rudely in the valley.
Soon her mouth began to fizz, filling with a residue
creamy as boot polish and everything pregnant with heat.
So the riddle of days, walking from doorstep to driveway
then back to school. *Disgusting*, my daughter said.
For at last the maggots came, teeming in the possum's
stopped, burned mouth. The air smelt of stewed semen,
the tongue like a black orchid, half-severed, dangled
and torqued. So the tongue swayed and in the fraying sleep
of my fatigue I could hear the quiet vowels, rising from
wisteria, from the hot ground, and falling back into silence.

NIGHT BIRDS

Snow falls undisturbed in branches. The city refuses
to dream for sparrows, for park drunks, though it's past
midnight. Like a prayer, our moon waits to be spoken.
Once we chased Mallarmé's swan, dragging dissolute
wings into flight. Winter's amnesia preserved us—
unearthly swans, writhing in mud. Words broke their
baroque chords creaking in my nest of bones. You wrote
me tempting alibis, singing the frost, blotting out stars.
Night birds slumber. Stay—with arms unhinged, we'll
watch sparks flame as dancing roses, souvenirs of silence.
My body rivers over absent fields, where words rescue
or reduce me until I try to erase whiteness, her artefacts—
a snow-dusted angel of the lake, the symmetry of elms
undressing like brides in the night's incomplete sentence.

ELIZABETH CAMPBELL

PROVERB

'In the room
where onions are frying
even the cat weeps.'

No more allegories – let's agree
proverbs help nobody.
No parables, I beg of you.

But then, who could love detail for its own sake?
Surely a gentle mind turns straight
away to symbol?

'Fact is the Kingdom of God.
Precision polishes the narrow heart.
Stories set us free.'

The enemies of complexity prefer such
companionable summaries.
But Mother Doubt, you early laid on me

your threefold cradle-gifts:
sadness, restlessness,
and foremost of these, a hopeless

passion of reality. And so
my beloved cat, weep.
No more parables – let's just disagree.

FEAR

I

Snake-man comes once a year; bare-foot
stamps and shouts, decanting snake after slow snake,
'A snake's near blind! He can't hear!'
Kids murmur and hush, knees touching
on the floor. 'You're rocks and plants to him!'

Inside their bursting stillness, empty
to soundless looping snake, who sees
only motion, each child – quiet Eurydice
and Orpheus of the loud mouth –
makes private truce with snake-fear: fear beyond myth,

beyond snakes' silent innocence of symbol,
far beyond venom and cure, as if the fang-hole
itself, or the naked waiting ankle were portal
to the death-world, the death-life:
where we live within fear of death as in a room.

II

World of the foal on his first day, who could not pass
the tarry plug in his gut; whom we held
hours in the scorching grass plunging and squealing,
and saved.

Heat and fear
were all his first knowledge, and our arms
the incomprehensible curb against
his earthly instinct to leap clear – . This earth

doesn't love you: earth
that would extinguish you in rock-fall fast
as air crushes the breath of the hooked fish
on its bed of sister-deaths. The same air that you gasp

when the liftshaft unlatches and throws you back
to the surface, air that is one giant breathing
mouth, a child's one example of abstraction
(unseen, untouchable): wind that tries to help you free

over every cliff to the ocean below: birth-waters, first
element, that started you, most of the world, most of your body,
the thousand-handed that would slide your lungs on
like a glove, then open its fingers, ending you.

       V *brain*
in here, the lurking flaw,
the tax, the glip, the twin, the mirror,
that fainted you away

from the party and further – two drags
on a joint and you drop and twitch and jerk
like a fish on the dry wharf and come up, six hours lost,

kidnapped, transported to the Old World
(History too, origin, is your fate, your grimacing Real)
to the red-and-gilt casino

the black-dressed war widow hunching over you
promising safety (now you know for certain
you are mad forever and never going home: you are home).

But really you're only out
ten seconds of mortal time and then the vision lurches
back to open-air and friends, cutting the music

/Thank god/ bending to you.

/did I wet myself?/throw up?/break my teeth?/

Quick warning, then continuance – you are
the dumb death-drive planted like a skull
in a Dutch portrait to ruin the party –

another night you drop in the back yard, thresh
ten seconds in a puddle, ruin your dress, falling
through your body, centre-of-earth,

to some mad kind of China – open your eyes
at the carnival in thrashed grass behind the tents,
all the shunting rides and lights flung up above

your splayed body, generator thumping
like the heart-and-dagger tattoos, roaring cock-rock
from the looming ferris-wheel, your fortune

locked in its topmost cage, plummeting,
until passing beanies with pitbulls stop and humble you
with common stranger-kindness (there's nothing they can do)

and suddenly are your scared friends and you –
snatched back from that up-ended finished you –
sit up, tremble apology, sip obediently

the proffered lukewarm cup. Who will believe
the lesson my grey brain taught, the intimate
wet ground, family with dogs?

DALKEY ISLAND

for Maria, David and Aingeal

Terns demonstrate the work of flight
by stopping in the sky – dropping
like flintheads to pierce the channel after prey:

turning the air-and-water beyond this cliff
with sudden decisions,
sheering off, thinking better, the way reasons

glance in our minds like flicks of sunny fish,
though mostly they miss – worrying
up again, riding another angle, until your reason

reasons suddenly: these powerful dives are powered
not by birds, but their agreement
with passive gravity.

Perhaps all your insights are this obvious –
modest freefalls out of doubt
when the mind stops beating and the head bows

out of the abstraction of the air, to whack fish
like nodding into sleep, terns plummeting
silently into the surface of giant seas,

JUSTIN CLEMENS

TRYING TO BUY THAT WHAT THEY HAVE NOT GOT

We don't have that kind said the girl so me and me trumpet got
a different kind altogether and gave her $5.00, where'pon
she looked politely at us, then said *sir, I need another 40 cents,*
which was the price of the original loaf we'd ordered
but they didn't have, so me trumpet fanfarared out *this one is only $4.60*
and I pointed to the board where the relevant legend was inscribed,
where'pon she, furious, slung our change back at us. Typical,
if someone give you something you don't want
they still try to charge you for what you did but didn't get,
and they'll have that only-too-familiar feeling of frustration,
garnished with a frisson of a sense of your injustice,
will that does not know, agon of fools, self-improvement as history,
progress no one wants nor can even envisage, swarming
reconciled by the ending-to-come, secularised providence,
and will-to-power already implying a field of competing forces
in which some of them simply fail to take it right to the bitter end.

WHIRL

It is not just the words you use, nor is
It what you would pretend our talk implies,
But that the air your mouth shapes with a kiss
To sense inspires such warmth in this disguise
That every sentence, like a tiny whirl
Of wind, tornado-like, blows in my ear
Those grains of sand that oysters turn to pearl,
If pearls indeed are things that one might hear.
And with those pearls, I would construct in mind
A necklace such as you have never seen;
And with stray laurels gathered on the wind,
I'll weave a coronet of living green
So that upon your brow and breast will twine
The coupled emblems of your love and mine.

DOWN

Come, come with me.

               A voice says,
there is no point at which your life was lost,
and unseasonable swallows plunge
headless into the void.

The dream again: milk steaming
in rivulets through striated mud
puddles for the cows to lap hoof-deep.
        The distances are wrong, awry
as if the surface were not flat
but incandescent with perceptions
that are not.
               Get up, get up now,
though you are dead
and go to the closest corpse to breath,
soft down cresting on the tongue
come like an eel to light, from depth.

MORNING

Dizzied from drink I wake in a grey morning,
peer through the curtains at the empty garden
where a cat stalks a bird. The bird too is grey.
I cannot remember if I still have a name.
Wherever you look, the world is blurring,
the bird is grey, the cat is purring,
the whole is shaking in the empty garden,
I have no name, all names are lacking,
the cat and bird are grey and wearing,
the morning too is grey, an awning
gaping on the days that coming
bring further cats and birds to further
farther meetings in far empty gardens.
I have no name. What comes is wearing
worldliness to fright and daring.
But grey birds sing and grey cats feed,
through song and meat propel the breed
to further song and meat in mornings
grey and empty, nameless. Yawning,
I have no name, the day is fawning
ever over grey birds squawking
in grey cats' claws in empty garden.
I have no name. There is no warding
to separate the caught from courting.
I have no name. The day is morning.

BALLADIA LIBIDINALIA

— among these drunk ambassadors of want
you cannot tell your haunting from your *honte* —
but must suspect their master's here to seize —
O — disquisitions of emissaries
to lose a mind to any mindless twitch
of slim electrodes' slimy-fingered switch —
the walls — before you even start to spasm —
bespattered horribly with oozing plasm —
inserting grimy little details in
your fat-arsed eyes like insects grimacing
at other's others' littering detritus —
like murderous fantasies' reclaimed refuse
to lick like dogs — where torn to tears in heat
or wriggle maggot-like in some old meat —
not one dry sprig untuned in these *châteaux*
be safe from writhing fingertips that hoe
each crinkled socket's orificial ring —
so sing — so sing — the whole un-focus-sing —
libid-o — ibid-o — bid-o — id-o — d-o — o — o — o — o

JOEL DEANE

GUANTANAMO

We saw.
Yet did not see.

The prefabricated cube of an isolation block
      plonked in the adventure playground
      could just have easily have been a toilet block.
The naked, hooded man menaced by
      Alsatians outside the delicatessen,
      a post-modern passion play.
The staged interrogations at the football oval—the crowd counting
      down the seventy-two point matrix for stress and distress—
      half-time entertainment.
The orange jumpsuits praying in cages placed at measured intervals
      along the median strip of the freeway,
      a promotional gimmick for commercial radio.
The pack of passenger airliners circling in the distance
      a vague disturbance of our equilibrium,
      like an unexplained thrum in the air conditioning.
The black hoods we took to wearing
      in the privacy of our bedrooms,
      a martial, but much needed, marital aid.

We saw.
Yet did not see.

Not even when, in the scrum of the stocktake sale, in menswear,
      we found three jumpsuits, mandarin orange and spattered red,
      hanging above a writhing pit of discount silk ties.

MAN TO WOMAN

after Judith Wright's 'Woman to Man'

Together, we belabour another night
without a timeless third to hold
who knows the lie of the final day—
silent, still, bereft of sight,
foregoes the harsh southern light.

There is no child, no mortal face;
no name we speak to say goodbye:
no sullen cherubim to kiss farewell.
Just the bones of heredity that we chase
without three children to embrace.

Theirs is a strength we will not know,
mouths that will not mouth your breast,
eyes that will not meet our eyes.
Theirs is a variant that no longer grows
(the most delicate of alpine rose).

This is the unmaking of what we made;
this is the answer without reply;
two untouchables in the unspeakable dark.
Who shines the light? Who wields the blade?
You hold me, and I am afraid.

DIVERTIMENTO

Viewing the body
in an open casket
of a blue plastic dish
on the linen fold
of a surgical mask—
as the unexpectant mother
            is wheeled away to theatre—
the newborns of St Vincent's
serenade our stillborn

with their cries.

I BUILD A LITTLE HOUSE WHERE OUR HEARTS ONCE LIVED

A master bedroom, a stripped mattress
dead centre of the floor.
Plastic dishes in the kitchen sink,
soft toys kicked against the wall.
Ikea furniture flat in boxes,
I assemble you without a key;
no need for Swedish instruction,
these hands know your symmetry.
Finished with bedevilled edges,
hewn from raw blonde pine,
inner suburban by desire,
Scandinavian by design.

I build a little house where our hearts
once lived—remake rooms I cannot find.

KATE
FAGAN

DADABASE

cento for Michael Farrell

Has genius ever spoken to you
about accordions? Neo-classicism discovers
mice. Paroxysm makes a trust
of all *artistic* cheeses, brr brrrrrr,
hello honey this is cinema. Consolidate
the harvest of exact calculations.
Art-parrot-word replaced by the new old
Wilde = foil
orphan = sunlight
gate = that
suffering = all
I wrote some poems tonight to go
with adbreaks to go with good reason.
Clearly there's an emergency, an Australian
treatment for belief. Why do we choose
such dark places for our books?
Fishing with *artistic* lines *btrp fretc*
rihh cantmmetr asot fipfthtngt
speaking from the depths what I heard
at the summit, my scarlet path
to infinite sainthood. Cue
Star Wars theme: *dada dadada dada*
dadada dada dadada da

A LITTLE SONG

cento for Ruby Minter

Before the world was blue
it was a little darker. The apple in a circle
by the bed, rain and all the birds.
Under sleep's care
you run run stop to sing
pleased with every accidental scene.
The first word. The first meadow
green, no dust and courage everywhere.
Moon O and sunlight O
the living fancy
cheered up yellow as peaches.
Wild house, the roof
a hammered silver fish-tail.
Rosy morning cry.

CONCRETE POEM

The beginning of duration
The infinity of cells
The form of unknowing
The hopelessness of dropped articles
The foot following the hand
The enticement of proclamations
The factual storm breaking between cables
The loss of a single throat
The particularities
The restaurant the satellite the city
The ambivalence of hours
The finity of care
The naming of difference
The reappearance of history
The violence in repetition in repeating
The repetition of ritual
The stealing light
The floor as we cross it
The unanswerable question of occurrence
The leaves the rivers the glass the dust
The absolute relevance
The petal as it falls
The book as it falls
The capital returning
The centralisation of numbers
The faces on ships and under fences
The domestic ear of infinite justice
The continuous event
The evening of a globe
The end of solid impossibility

LETTER IV: ON REALITY

We crossed the seaward field
with the air heavy against us,
our heels mining canticles from clay.
Look, you said, this is real.
The boats decay on their painters
and no one lives to sail them.
Later I saw a woman walking
past us with a lamp, illuminating

nothing but the stones
that lay broken under our feet.
I wanted suddenly to understand
the world's darker evidence,
as though the raw wager of death
skilled our souls for a greater yield.

LETTER XI: AGAPE (REPRISE)

Where is the sky? My heart is a metal clock.
Why are you going? To find sound.
How can I begin? Every wheel rolls to nowhere.
Then you are lost. This song is my only requirement.
Will you come back? My skin longs for the blue promise of sun.
Where is the picture? Inside the painter.
What do you hear? Only the blood in my eardrums.
And what do you seek? The colour of strangeness.
How do the hours fly? As a hawk: straight to the mountain.
Who will count the days? I will leave a word for every step.
And the years? A green dress by a red well.
What do you mean? Knowledge breaks like a first bud.
How will you remember? Light will come slowly.
I loved you in darkness. We are more than ourselves.

JANE

GIBIAN

TIDEMARK

you begin here: part of a distant beach
missing its home, a doll's saucerful
of the cleanest sand sleeping in your ear

grown into something with glairy edges,
a tidemark advancing and receding less
with the disintegration of arctic sea ice

affirmed when you accidentally cut
the pale baby capsicum forming inside
its dark red mother, the centre of a world

to turn around: beneath the surface
dark rocks loom in the glassy water,
further out, mutable peaks of white froth
tease your eyes with dolphins

where you end: that part of the beach
pining for home, and at the centre
an instrumental continuo around which
all other voices circle and rub

SOUND PIECE

Geometric rows of drawers in the curiosity cabinet,
and hidden compartments that open onto imprecise
chronometry: in the top left, gardens of giant kelp

seething and gurgling against mottled orange rocks;
traces of seaweed and decomposition. The next drawer
slides open to the sound of rain without it, and the plinking

of flags blowing against flagpoles. Too hazardous,
holding the specimens still enough to pin firmly through
their torsos. A weathered tray replays the rhythmic note

of a baby sister sucking her dummy in the night,
heard as measured adult steps in the bushy darkness
beyond the sliding glass door. Another drawer holds

the slicing of a green apple into wafers with the worn
brown knife. In a middle compartment: the swish
of a letter dropped into the post box; an unaccompanied

motet, forty voices wide, rising into dense layers
of amplitude to fill the many-spaced time-piece,
its fallible classification. A lower drawer consists

of walking into the threads of old spider webs, and
the distant grumble of a bus arriving at last. This section
for sea creatures: the skeleton of a small fish, fossilised

with eerie blank eyes and slender barbel; the graduated
spiral of a shell so perfect it doesn't seem real, then
a stripe of sunlight across our shins, leading

to a shelf that preserves the pang of a muted light
gleaming from the windows of your last house.

CONTINUITY

We've been looking for the not old, the not new,
as it is held by a gloved hand with four different-coloured
fingers which open onto emptiness. We're slow moving
to the smudged isometric rings from the bottoms of cups
on a sticky table, and I've been having trouble with articles;
now isn't definite or indefinite but seems to fit in one inhalation,
a poem that rides the wave of a single breath and holds
the hypnotic taste of a handstand in the mouth.

I'm experimenting with the past and a present that's
continuous and perfect: the poppies have already spat
their furry green coats into the room from their superior
position on the mantelpiece, and they aren't holding on
to something nameable like a gloved hand. It's not
nameable, waking to the slither of a hairbrush
through long hair; there was nothing more to be had.

We've been inhabiting the second-person, or I've been
trying: sliding a clip into your hair while holding the other
in your mouth; knowing the image well and how dwelling
in it feels. Nothing more: birds perched on a telephone line,
evenly spaced and still as sculptures, a frozen moment scarcely
reachable, and the strings of a scratchy hesitant Shostakovich
hovering like a honeyeater are appearing and vanishing;
we're being left with an absence more than touchable.

PARTS OF THE TONGUE

A predilection for stone fruit
sees a trail of peach
and plum stones in his shadow
You had traced him down
this discreet path to where
his casual touch
                  was six light insect
feet on your forearm

In the magazine you read about
the ten sexiest women
for April; they all live
in suburbs beginning with W
and wear impossible shoes

You hunt for modern equivalents
of *One Hundred Ways with Mince*
and watch his hand become
refined under its wedding ring,
the fingers longer and nails less bitten

He coaxes your shoulders straight,
uncurling them with firm hands

but you were merely bent over
with laughter
Now your tongue forks into four:
one part for being good-natured
        one for lamentation
               the third part of irony
and the last for an imaginary language

You move to a newly invented
suburb beginning with X
where you will use the four parts
of the tongue with equilibrium

ARDENT

Có gì đó lướt trên nụ cười lưỡi dao
Như thiên nga lướt mộng mị trên mặt hồ tỏ a sóng

Something glides on the smile of the knife
Like a swan dreamily skimming the surface of the lake

Nguyễn Quang Thiều,
'Eleven Parts of Feeling'

You wanted everything, to hold it all: the precise
measure of tears filling each eye, to ingest
parts of a concerto into the body: you want
a locked box for the scraps of paper, that recipe

of ideas; a treasure chest to quarantine your heart –
but already it's the time of dahlias, the ending
of the time of sunflowers; almost the reign
of goannas, when the birds call unmistakeable

warnings to one another. You needed to zoom in
so closely a sprig of lavender became myriad
tiny blooms bursting in spirals; you had to lick
the knife blade. Waking cut like a sword,

clambering from the dream of a soldier leaving –
she was pressing her cheek against the cotton chest
of a tall man, faceless, inhaling serenity and amaranth;
the lull, the surrender into a dark smudge of sleep.

The ardent harbour exploding with infinite stars:
you tried to hold it all – like the knife between
your teeth, it's a trapdoor into the night now:
under the clipped fingernail of a moon, you find
yourself staring straight into the eyes of an owl.

SUMMER SEQUENCE

stepping carefully
between pointed gumnut caps –
your bare feet

late sunlight
spider threads
join two leaves to a grass blade

black moths
flutter in the garage:
we look for an old cricket bat

cool change
long sheets of bark
twist through the air

saucers of seedpods
on the dinner table –
one bursts open under the light

all evening
the slow swish of bat wings
in flowering gums

LISA
GORTON

DREAMS AND ARTEFACTS

after the Titanic Artefact Exhibition

I.
Patiently, ticket by ticket, a soft-stepped crowd
advances into the mimic ship's hull half-
sailed out of the foyer wall, as if advancing into
somebody else's dream –
the interior, windowless, where perspex cases bear,
each to its single light, small relics –
a tortoiseshell comb, an ivory hand mirror,
a necklace pricked with pin's head costume pearls.
They might be mine – at least, things loosed
from a dream I had, off and on, for years.
They have suffered nothing, these things raised
from a place less like place than like memory itself –

II.
Where the sea is
worked back upon itself in soundless storm,
        a staircase climbs.
Its scroll of iron foliage grows in subtler garlands now –
it is the sea's small
machinery of hunger, feeding on iron, makes these
        crookedly intricate festoons,
as if it were the future of remorse – Piece by piece,
the staircase returns
                to the conditions of dream.

III.
In the next room, they have custom-built a staircase.
A replica, reinvented from a photograph,
it leads nowhere – or it leads to the house of images
where nothing is lost. A clock without a mechanism
adorns its first floor landing, hands stopped at that minute
history pours through. We forgive things
only because we own them – This is a staircase
not for climbing, its first step strung with a soft-weave rope.

IV.
It is raining as I leave –
long rain breaking itself onto the footpath,
breaking easily into the surface of itself
like a dream without emblems, an in-drawn shine.
Overhead, clouds build and ruin imaginary cities,
slow-mo historical epics with the sound down,
                    playing to no one.

THE HUMANITY OF ABSTRACT PAINTING

for Diena Georgetti

I.
Afternoon rain on the windows,
bare rooms stilled with light – an idea of the house
that had always haunted your life in it,
as if to say This is the machine of the present.
It reinvents experience as a daydream.
This is the empty house –

II.
The rain sound is less like sound
than it is the trick of familiar places, which return
things to the conditions of imagery.
Boxes filled with what you own. Now
room after room you make this more entire
architecture of memory –

III
An infinite of loss closed
in its frame like the house of a modernist: furniture
fit to the room. Everything thought, every thing
remembered, as if somebody else's house
now has you in it, a collector of things as they were
in somebody else's dream –

IV.
Because a collector is free
as facing mirrors prove the renewal in what it is
to be possessed. Rooms you could walk through
blind, windows of rain-coloured light.
This is the house that silence returns to you.
This is the empty house.

MISTLETOE

for Rebecca Mayo

A subtler haunting, as mistletoe
subdues its leaf to the host, possessed
by what it feeds on – Still
its lopsided chandelier flourishes
on the stricken branch where self-
defeating pride, dignity's withdrawn
sad smile, furnish no room.
Upon necessity's crooked vaulting –
that drawn-out bewilderment
called making do – it offers up
its ripe berry, its indigestible seed.

THE AFFAIR

Our last illicit weekend,
a little tired and driving
to some Blue Mountain
getaway or other.
On the motorway
it is the car that overheats
                    whoosh
I think a whale is
caught in our engine.
We wait in the car
trying to feel
absolute about each other.
They all drive past.

LIBBY

HART

IN DEVELOPMENT

This has somehow
become a clandestine affair
that burns holes through nightfall

Yet as hot and heavy as this may sound
there's still the freezing of trees
that snap clean
against a hard edge
of a lonely road,
slicing the gutter up
with useless timber.

But even in the wintering
I am able to recognise your form,
to watch its shifting shape
as it transgresses.

And I've decided that it's you I have faith in,
more so than what measurement I can give.
It's you, who stops on the edge of thought
while I rummage through restlessness.
It's you, who is growing determined,
who is learning to speak your mind.

THE DREAM JAR

This jar made of glass and heavy with cloud
throbs to the touch
like a deer I have startled it.
Heartbeats press into the palm of my hand.

I watch it as if it were a film
keep an eye on its clouds
see how a forest of them turns sharply into sky
then into portraits
which hang deep inside cumulus form.

Actions occur in silence
a tight lid holds conversations well
but there isn't much to tell –
words are just air with meanings.

Untouchable syllables
ooze through skin, sentences pass into fingerprints.
Rain begins to fall.

I see my dream of snails inside each drop of rain –
one million snails in the garden.
With the morning light approaching
I stand with bare feet on the path
as they ride my toes as hills.

LONE FIGURE – *MALIN HEAD*

The wind talks of its travels
and the muse's head turns to listen.

And its wildness is something remembered,
as if long, long ago it clung to me.

And it is wild-reaping. It's the future coming at us –
the past loitering, loitering a little bit too long.

And it is distance, and does not sew its sides together.
Instead, it leaves the measurement as is:

horizon without trace of you, and
these eyes searching and never getting close.

And my head is in the ocean,
full of splashes. I'm fleet-footed

as the weather turns sharp as cut stone.
It blades my face and all that it touches.

WOMAN DRAWING THE CURTAINS OF HER BEDROOM – *CARRICK-ON-SHANNON*

My thoughts are with you tonight,
they belong where your feet walk.

They go down to the river
its bend, the curve of serpent
slunk beneath.

Body of water,
a wetness, sucking. A splash, a drop.
Her belly swollen and swallowing,
sinking down with a swish of tail.

Blubbing and lugging
this weighted island-world,
a push of girth
netting our own wet bodies
of muscle and tide,
the heart-thump of land
unanchored below feet.

This *island of the ocean*,
how it sways us to sleep
with its breath of undertow,
its guardians of storm above our heads.

Their hint of speech falls on sodden ground,
near-words reach me.

LONE FIGURE – *ANNAGHMAKERRIG*

Down the hill I went
watching the weak outline of all things
inside a soft rain.

      And in the distance came the lake's presence,
a kind of shimmer standing there like longing.

      And in the distance a small movement approached me.

It scuttled in patches of light
and when it reached me it was eager for touch.
A black and white cat, we made polite conversation
then went our separate ways.

      And when I reached the lake
the night had become all but dripping trees.

      And I stood underneath these tears
trying to make sense of something.

I listened hard, listened to the soft edges of the water
move inside a sway so like vocation.

      And I thought of water spirits rising,
of leaves dripping and a lake lapping.

I looked out towards O'Hanlon's Hill
and the world felt very small
as if I could put it in my pocket,
rub it like a polished stone.

WIDOWER SITTING ON THE EDGE
OF HIS BED – *KINSALE*

Your presence embraces all things today.
Trees are talking to the wind,
birds call your name. Clouds look like angels.

I remember how you tasted like honey
inside a day of amber.
These curtains, how they trembled like wings.

WOMAN – *BRAY HEAD*

Those words you used, how they cleaved me
to an ache that shaped a wave.

Now I find myself travelling as a wet bundle.

All my fingers have become droplets,
my mind stumbles through a whirl of fish.

And as the shoal turns, I in turn draw nearer to you.

I'd held the phone like a shell, imagining
a bedside light curving your face while you spoke.

That's when the dripping began, the falling to a splash.

Now I find myself seeking sea legs to stand up in.
I stretch and reel into nautical mile

as you bathe in the dawn, as I drink the night.

SARAH HOLLAND-BATT

THIS LANDSCAPE BEFORE ME

Is unwritten, though it has lived in violence.

First the factory stood, quiet as an asylum.
Then the annihilating mallee with its red fists of blossoms
and the mountain ash creeping over it like a stain.

I have no proof, but I tell you
there were leadlight windows here once, barred.
They cast a little striped light on the women.

Now in scrub and yellow broom I stand on a history
braided and unbraided by stiff Irish wrists.
The rope and span and carded wool are unpicked
as are their faces and names.

Londonderry, Cork, Galway, Kildare –
as I say the words they are sucked away
to a hemisphere in darkness.

I will not presume to say
what suffering is or how it was meted out in this place.
At what point it breaks a body I cannot tell.

But this morning I saw a young rabbit
hunched in brush and shadow.
I saw its lesioned face, its legs too thin to scramble,
the blood-berry red and pink scab of its eye.

It had caught the disease
we brought here for it
and wanted a quiet place to die.

And it was lucky, or as lucky as it would get –
there was time and light, the hawks and dogs
had not been written yet, and were still out of sight.

THE ORCHID HOUSE

Pegged under banana trees,
our backyard hothouse was fixed summer
that boiled all year, a green humpy
breathing gauze in meshy sheets.
Indoors it poured artificial rain.

Under that striped sunlight
I crept the spider-heavy shelves
where exotics festered in their Latin names.
I torqued the twist-wires tight
around each trumpeting neck,
chivvied longlegs from potted dark
as outside the clouds blew back like years.

My grandfather spoke a strange pidgin in there,
knew Cat's Face from Queen of Sheba,
Snake Flower, Soldier's Crest, Sulphur Tail.
A decade late, I found a wrinkled block of newsprint
under the orange crucifix,
six men waist-deep in the Mekong
where the war's end could never come.

Death never reached those suburbs, not really.
Bodies in their Sunday Best
never lay on our cool kitchen table
stiff as celluloid dolls,
and last goodbyes
were told by nurses in chemical code.

When Grandad died, the wonky shack
grew wild, and creepers curtained over.
Through walls thin and threadbare

I heard them hissing, the cold wet tendrils
which could strangle, and grew on air:
teatree, tangle root, tongue.

NIGHT SONNET

Speak softly now: the neighbours are sleeping.
Cars drowse under the window quiet as mousetraps,
smoke winds up silently from an ashtray
like the plumes of a deep sea squid,
a grit of light trembles on our white bedsheets.
Who are you beside me, irresolute
as a flag in the wind, your face gliding
into wolfish dreams, your breath dragging
like a styrofoam cup in the street?
I like watching you like this, running
bodiless through the alleys of a foreign city,
hunted by the sound of a stranger's coat.
The stone tilts – spears of blue shadow.
The stairs are steep, there is nowhere to go.

THE SEWING ROOM

My mother measured the margins
of my known world there:
a sunlit annex where the lines converged,
wrist to shoulder-blade, hip, ankle, waist;
maps I would only outgrow
charted in painstaking tailor's chalk.

Under her foot, the Singer roared;
sometimes a foxtrot, sometimes a waltz,
she treadled the pedal with a pianist's touch.
Cotton silos undressed into breakneck zeds
along the pocket of a Liberty print skirt
as I scavenged the rag-bag on cork
for grizzled silk, a paisley cuff.

Cabin-feverish, I toyed
with toggles and bobbins to the sprung
rhythm of that flying silver foot,
jackhammering, runaway metal
stitching a puzzle of buttonholes and pleats.
So many weekends remaindered, and for what?
A skirt? You wore it; you took it off.

What did I know of making then,
rearranging a few sad odds and ends
under my mother's pinned smile,
her teeth interspersed with ersatz pearl?
The overlocker zagged on like a lie-detector test.
I kept watch. It never leapt.

THE ART OF DISAPPEARING

The moon that broke on the fencepost will not hold.
Desire will not hold. Memory will not hold.
The house you grew up in; its eaves; its attic will not hold.
The still lives and the Botticellis will not hold.
The white peaches in the bowl will not hold.
Something is always about to happen.
You get married, you change your name,
and the sun you wore like a scarf on your wrist has vanished.
It is an art, this ever more escaping grasp of things;
imperatives will not still it – no *stay* or *wait* or *keep*
to seize the disappeared and hold it clear, like pain.
So tell the car idling in the street to go on;
tell the skirmish of chesspieces to go on;
tell the scraps of paper, the lines to go on.
It is winter: that means the blossoms are gone,
that means the days are getting shorter.
And the dark water flows endlessly on.

LK HOLT

THE CHILDREN AND THE WORLD

The children go to school and they come back
they walk as a procession of little monarchies
their daily orbits inscape the world
The children go to school and they come back
the world bites them at their shiny heels
the morning sun chooses every girl
The children go to school and they come back
there's much audience for the animal feats of boys
proficient in front of the fathers of the world
The children go to school and they come back
pondering the logical invalidity of siblings
the impossibility of shared matter and toys
The children go to school and they come back
they thread through bus-stop crowds ducking
away from the swing of hands deadly-jewelled
The children go to school and they come back
thrown loose on the world like homing pigeons
and returning in miracles modest and midafternoon

FALSE STARTS

Take the exquisite sleeve of my ritual kimono
and wipe your mouth on it. We'll both just fit
in the horse carcass to outlast the blizzard.
Our pelvises jangle like a god's game of jacks.
You would reach the station in time to save me,
being punctual ordinarily. The clear blood
of the blood of me is profusely, transfusely,
yours. We are tarred by the same warm brush.
Head knocking bedhead, an ascetic little prayer.
Light and air flush open the gothic vault
behind the face. Red not a colour but ajar.

(Like this she passes the winter, Penelope,
the weathers outside the window, the bare twigs
hard in their belief in the bud's true start.)

GIRLS

The perfected ingénue turns straight into woman;
the feather-moult, the piecework undone to do again.
Is the Child killable enough to start from scratch—
the adolescent, a blithe Fury with bored shears?

I ask for the sake of June. Her magnified eyes
inspired us to the hard petrified names of animals;
both the totem and its sacrifice. She talked to no one
but herself. I was left at June's house one day,

told to play quietly or else June might have a turn.
She proffered her tortoise; I patted the air above
its death-mask shell. We took it to sleep in the grass
as we swung on the swings; pink, earnest pendulums.

June took a flying dismount, her glasses shuck-light,
the shell-crack a horror, the cracked shell a heraldry—

PORTRAIT WITH RED BIRD

She stands, an old matter of fact, at the restroom mirror.
Her husband rings from their table and asks *what's taking so long*.
She stares at herself as she answers *must you know all*:
not a question. Must it always be so visible (the real question)
her insides art. She thinks of all the preceding reds on whites,
seals still warm; schooldresses, marriage sheets, and now this
little wound of red wine on her blouse. Her hand over it like
the Egyptian amulet: two obsidian fingers, slightly parted,
holding closed the incision where the organs were let out.

A cage shook empty out the window of her dying mother's house,
the king parrot waking up from its fall and flying off.

FROM INSIDE THE MRI SCANNER

Conveyed headfirst on a slab, I feel a terror
wilfully dumb: I'm wrongly being put in the furnace.
I mistake sound for heat, then for nothingness;
inkling of bone-scree picked out of a sift-pan
for the urn. Though something remains in my eyelids
twitching, then the bass-nerve in rapture goes:
the brain receives and uninspired calls it pain.

All sensation is for the life-form's good!
this thrum of the hydrogen I'm custodian of,
these atoms rousing like Great Birnam Wood;
I keep actively still like a king in view.
Why do I remember the wretchedness
of bobbing for apples? When I rise my smile
is a primate's grimace, eyes extraneous—

EMMA JONES

TIGER IN THE MENAGERIE

No one could say how the tiger got into the menagerie.
It was too flash, too blue,
too much like the painting of a tiger.

At night the bars of the cage and the stripes of the tiger
looked into each other so long
that when it was time for those eyes to rock shut

the bars were the lashes of the stripes
the stripes were the lashes of the bars

and they walked together in their dreams so long
through the long colonnade
that shed its fretwork to the Indian main

that when the sun rose they'd gone and the tiger was
one clear orange eye that walked into the menagerie.

No one could say how the tiger got out in the menagerie.
It was too bright, too bare.
If the menagerie could, it would say 'tiger'.

If the aviary could, it would lock its door.
Its heart began to beat in rows of rising birds
when the tiger came inside to wait.

CONVERSATION

'Oh this and that. But for various reasons' –
(the season, and the change in season, the season of grief

and retrospection, the rooftop pulled from the childhood
house, and the internal doll in its stuck seat,

that is, the fictive soul in its brute cathedral, and because of memory,
maybe, and organs in niches, and the beat to things,

and the knowledge that the body is the soul and vice versa,
but that false distinctions are sometimes meaningful,

and that difference, all difference, is just distance, not a state,
not a nation, and because nothing *matters*, not really,

or everything does, I don't mind being an animal, at all,
because a sentient thing is nothing else, and because toward matter

I feel neither love nor hate but the kind of shuttered
swiss neutrality a watch might feel for time

if it had an animal's sentiments, knowing itself a symbol
and function, knowing itself a tool, and because I feel

the dull culmination of various phenomena informing me
and am that culmination, I feel ill in some small way,

though not ill really, just idle, and I prefer, you see,
to keep an impassive inviolable pact with things that tick,

with solitary, shifted things, and because my life's approximate act
is the sister to some other life, with different tints, I carry

and nurse, my diffident twin, I'm often morose, and think
of those statues that lean above themselves in water,

those fountains, stone, with commemorative light,
with disfiguring winds, and because reflection is an end in itself

and because there's an end even to reflection, and an end to the eye,
that heated room, I prefer to keep my artifice and my arsenal

suspended, close; like an angled man; like the stationed sun;
and because matter ends, or I should say, matter turns to matter,

and my small inalienable witness to this is real, I can't pretend
to wish to be a rooted thing, full-grown, concerned

with practical matters, in a rooted world, and careful of borders,
when an ineradicable small portion glints, my mind, that alma mater,

and says, make your work your vicarage) – 'I put off going back'.

PARADISE

What you wanted was simple:
a house with a fence and a kind of gulled
light arching up from it to shake in the poplars
or some other brand of European tree
(or was it American?) you'd plant
just for the birds to nest in and so
the crows who'd settle there
could settle like pilgrims.

Darling, all day I've watched the garden make its way
down the road. It stops at the houses
where the lights are on and the hose reel is tidy
and climbs to the windows to look inside
like a child with its eyes of flared rhododendrons
and sunflowers that shutter the wind like bombs
so buttered and brave the sweet peas gallop
and the undergrowths fizz through the fences
and pause at some to shake into asters
and weep.

The garden is a mythical beast and a pilgrim.
And when the houses stroll out it eats up
their papers and screens their evangelical dogs.

Barbeque eater,
yankee doodle,
if the garden should leave
where would we age
and park our poodle?

'This is paradise,' you said,
a young expansive American saint.
And widened your arms to take it in,
that suburb, spread, with seas in it.

PAINTING

Everyone's souls, which didn't exist, were playing up,
and they flocked as the shadows we left on the ground
when the tired sun – that midday man – was an artist.
And they surfaced in the sweat that made for us
a soft and lunar garment worn abroad, an outline,
and a second skin. The inside out, and the outside in –

And still the light comes, and into the eye,
and with it a world, and a borderland.
And you set your easel between the rocks
and you painted the way a man might paint
if he weren't a man, but a dismal bird
that saw below him stretched a dismal bird-
land, filled with wind, and with white paper,
and made of beautiful, counterfeit birds –

Such glyphs, such strokes
the gathered arabic
of themselves, their wings
those folded homes
as each dull sail,
dull soul, takes off.

And you said 'every memory's a motel.'
(Dull soul, dull sail.)
And death was a breezy man who arranged
and rearranged the birds and branches and
'can the clouds continue until evening?'
you said, perched upon the classical rocks,
apish and pale, claw-footed, like a bath.

And the canvas said 'there's no division,
just a vision forced of earth and sky.'
While the painting leaned out, forgetful,
and made the day in its own image.

have the same look, of something surprised.
But, at the same time, not surprised at all –

A vacancy, over which the stripes ride,
in a fictive jungle, and ministered

by Delacroix, who heats the vacancy.
Or by whoever found the tiger in

my 1950s three-toned textbook
trees and drew it out.

This illustration needs no root.
Stripes create the tiger for the eye;

the gallery wall hosts melanin shadows;
I have a plastic tiger on my desk finds prey in nothing
but the vacancy of shuttered windows.

I saw a copy of a copy once.
It was a Chinese painting, post-war;
in it, the tiger stands on a mountain,

looking out. Snow threatens him. His stripes
bead and sag. In the distance, a grey town.

The caption reads: 'the tiger has something on his mind'.
And in the commentary the tiger

is 'the symbol of the muffled artist'.
In the sky, a Communist

Creator leans, bearded and delicate,
through stilled winds, and the tiger stands, present;

and resolutely absent, too, looking
out onto nothing but an absence of tigers.

Snow is a philosophy. It paints tigers.
And the tiger has nothing on its mind.

DANIJELA KAMBASKOVIC-SAWERS

A MIGRANT WRITER ON A BUS
(THINKING OF KUNDERA)

The body crosses over quickly,

but characters stay behind
and roam ghosted streets.

Shuffling their feet,
they look for shops no longer there

and squabble urgently
in an inaudible language.

Should one make an effort
and force stories out

or allow the body to just sit,
invisible,

amidst its irrelevant geography
and enjoyable clutter,

and let the imagination
migrate at its own pace,
a language an eon?

The outward gaze
compares tree shapes to remembered trees
colours of landscape to imprinted colours

drinks from surrounding faces
to quench old thirsts
kindle new tastes

the invisible parallels unfurl
to tape-measure the distance
between us and us
between home and home.

RAPUNZEL TO THE PRINCE

3

This box contains
everything you need
to start a fascinating hobby.

Your real life
under a black curtain

in moving images
and silver threads
woven through the grey

waiting
for a slant of light

squeezed hard
through the eye of the needle:

the spite of sweet relief.

This box contains
everything you need
to start a fascinating hobby:

a fold of skin, an turn of an ankle
a screw
a warm pad

a secret place
where dream and memory
drink of each other;

a lover-sage
a fact-filled page
to take you through.

Make your own
fill your own
get started now.

5

Of course we'll fork and spoon. But then, let's knife.
Just split the groove at knife-point. Cut the wrist
when tied too hard, and kiss the welt, my life,
and take my point. Feel free to smile and twist:
I know your eyes. No fear. I'll lick the blade—
the smooth, the rough; I'll look for sharper treasure;
your jack-knife's-in-the-box; your spade's a spade,
you give a smoky uppercut of pleasure;
let's knife, my dear. Your cutting edge rings true.
Let rip the bloated skin, the viscous stream,
unleash that smoothest sigh. It splits the shoe.
Your teeth marks, rivets, hooks; the punch, the seam,
I want it all. Let's knife. Let's scream. Let's sue.
Let others sing of peace. I'll live the dream.

THE WILLIAD
THE EPIC ON THE EPIC, *ÉCRITURE FEMININE*

The Writer and the Monsters
of Child and Housework

The first victory hers, the Writer thought,
she would now write her epic. But as she went
to get a coffee, the Growing Pile of Dishes
stabbed her in the eye, and the Toilet Bowl
let out a murky howl. Its voice was drowned
by the cacophony of Dirty Sheets
begging for change. Then the dread Soiled Washing
squirmed in its basket, teemed and churned, growling,
while Dinner spat chips, rattled the fridge-cage
and pushed its fishy fingers towards her.
Fencing with each of these Monsters in turn,
the Writer tripped on toys littering the floor
and groped for balance. A shelf of books
fell on her foot, launching pointy corners
straight into her flesh. "Tidy your room!"
she screamed, tearful. "Later," grumbled the Child,
"I want to watch TV now." The Writer
cajoled; then, toys away, read four stories,
and, later that night, changed some peed-on sheets.

RETURN TO KALEVALA

I will lie down
tired of travel

let my hair grow slowly
wind along the river bed

A silver lake
rippling beneath me
a fairy language
wailing inside me

the bird of time
will land on my knee
and lay a hot
iron egg

I'll jerk my knee
and out of the broken egg
a world will grow

BRONWYN
LEA

TWO WAYS OUT

One way out of the insufferable
medium of a par-boiled heart

is to desire desire until your lungs
expand like a universe

light years away from implosion.
Forget this wanting a little a lot

of things (or its converse), aim
to want it all – the red dress, red shoes

the body with its yellow fat and red
muscle shifting your mysterious bones.

Another way out is to exhale,
to toss everything until you are left

with only a desire to toss things out –
get rid of that, too. Tell the world

it can't fire you because you've quit,
say *Self, sit till you no longer want*

to blaze in paradise. Stand in
the corner until each thought is

a fly crawling across the white wall
of your flesh. Whether

you walk the ascetic alley –
barefoot on the dead tufted earth

or gape inside the rococo theatre –
your hands parting the velvet curtain

step out, step through, meet me
out back. I'll be the one who is smiling.

ANTIPODES

In this lifetime *antipodes* must be my word,
my home or anyone else's. Anyone who lives
at opposites or knows what it is to be contrary,
to deviate. Like disparate continents.
Like the holding of Europe and Australia
in your blood. This, I find, is a feat.
And I recognise as I age that my apogees
are elongating, my reversals are rising
like the swollen belly of a frog storing water
in its sleep. My friend feels it too and wonders
if she can ever love down to the lonely and beyond;
beyond that rocky, existential space that women
like us, so schooled in ricochet, retreat from
with the swiftness of a silver-capped bullet.
There is a man I know with eyes heavy
with sand and sometimes sullen blue like
the haze of the eucalypt grove that makes
you remember all the f-words you never use
like *forgiven* and *forever*. He has grown on me
like an embryo until without him I feel thrown
into being incomplete like the wintering
rose bush de-leafed and out of bloom;
like the falling apart mountain, a mountain
that all my tying together won't mend.
Then just now, lying in the low light
of afternoon, I saw it is the movement
more than the man that I love; the movement
in and out of me, framing the sweet falling
of lilac pollen, falling soft upon his back,
my tongue.

THE CHINESE FOOT

The bandage wraps figure eights
around her heel, across the crest
of her foot and tightly over her toes
(which are black and pressed
to her sole) so that her arch breaks
magnificently with the steep pitch
of a temple. She lets her husband
touch it. He uses the measure
of his thumbtip-to-first-knuckle
along her lily foot and counts one,
two, three and smiles. He brings it
to his lips, inhales, and thanks
the ancestors, who also smile
and wish him many sons. He has
loved her since first he saw her,
swaying in the courtyard like
a little tree, her long braid blue
under the moon, her lily feet
dressed in green apple silk shoes.
His mouth fell open at the sight,
but he was careful when he
exhaled not to blow her over
with the white cloud of his breath.

THE NIGHTGOWN

dream is reason turned inside out
so we see daylight's other side

or is it the other way round –
reason is dream turned inside out

as the Japanese woman in her desire
turns her nightgown inside out

to dream of her absent lover –
constructs of seams and loose threads

facing the world, the seeming seamless
elision of silk against her skin

in daylight she watches her body age
the long rains are falling

commits to a life of dreaming –
whether the lover appears or he doesn't

whether their meeting is fruitful or isn't –
the black shell of night is a nut or is not

THE FLOOD

What do they know of war
it's the summer of 1938
and they're smiling on a beach
in Tenby, Wales. History
hasn't happened yet, though Freud's
rocked up in London, Superman debuted
in Action Comics #1, and Roosevelt
has commenced his fireside chats.
But it's a dazzling black and white
chromogenic day in Tenby, and Frank
is solid in white linens,
sleeves rolled up, Havana at hand,
sand scalloping his white patent shoes.
Elsie leans in for a kiss,
tanned in a halter top and shorts,
she touches his forearm
with an intimate lightness that reveals
no knowledge of the future – at least
that's how I remember

the photograph
as it sat near a century away
on my window sill in Brisbane,
Australia. Now I kneel
at a bathtub and everywhere
around me faces stare up
from the mud. Frank and Elsie
float into the present. I wash them
with my thumbs as tenderly
I washed sleep from the eyes
of their granddaughter and a huge red
beam, curtain of fire, Aurora

Australis, blooms across Wales,
lighting up their lives from the other side
of death. And the brain can discern
the different scales of loss –
it's paper in my hands not flesh –
but the heart, the biological
heart – how my heart pounds
at what it takes, and almost hopes,
is history's end.

BORN AGAIN

After the divorce he sold his house
by the beach & drove his Volkswagen
into the desert to die. He was gone
a year. I was living one vertical mile
above the desert floor – where he slept
in his car – in a house that overlooked
a great sweep of rocks & woodlands.
Instead of dying, god spoke to him.
God forgave all of his trespasses. But I
Didn't forgive his trespasses against me.
My heart was a long ledger. One day
he returned to collect our daughter.
My house was snowbound. I left him
To stand in the weather while I gathered
her things. It took a little while. When
I returned he was gone. Typical.
I looked around. Sparrows scratched
at the snow looking for seeds. I saw
a figure kneeling by a large granite
boulder. The ponderosa above him
was weighted with snow. The knees
of his jeans were wet. Snow drifts
on his shoulder & backs of his shoes.
Snow collected on his upturned palms.
I felt its coldness. Such intimacy
we had never shared. Sometimes grace
comes like that, it falls like snow.

CAMERON LOWE

THE SUM

for Tess

Already the world
is waiting for you.

Loaves,
discs of sun,

moth wings drifting
through an ancient night.

The sum
of all imaginings

rests in you,
seeds glowing

in the warm dark,
a deep music

circling your heart.
There's a song

to sing you forth
into this screaming light;

forgive us as we sing it.

SOMETHING LIKE A LEAF

The leaf is the size of a man's hand turning
in the breeze, turning through the cool light
at the edge of summer to which sparrows
give voice as dawn unwinds. Find it there,
beside the blue flowers of the twisting vine,
by the rose that blooms pink then red
above the fence-line that is the limit of sight
from the precise angle of . . . Find it swaying
in the clean promise of things to come,
of which you might say: *she will give grace*
that bore the printed flower—each birth,
each death in this garden, a proven law.
Find it in any manner that summons
that rich texture that is nothing like the feel
of the silk she wears close to her skin,
nor the feel of her skin that wakes you
in the night. Find it completely by surprise,
noting the perfect symmetry of veins
that glow a bright lime when the sun
turns the corner of the house where she
wanders dreaming in the gift of sleep. Find it,
noting its shape that is something like a heart
but more comely, something like a thought
but more defined, something nurtured
at the margins of the leaf itself.

MORNING LIGHT

Memory, surrender, all the sweet
seductions of regret—
last night's clothing tangled
on a chair, shadows
shifting on the bedroom wall.
Quietly, insistently, rehearse
the words: *nothing grand—*
the scale is neither big nor small.
Through the slats of the blinds
the light drives in and the shadows
change shape, change again.
When she gardens, a sky-blue scarf
holds back her hair. Remember?

Drifting with the sea sounds, rubber
hissing across bitumen, little waves
of abstraction as the morning,
devoid of ambition, simply occurs.
And do you also listen to the birds?
Magpies, pigeons, sparrows—
they've been at it for hours.
And do you still step from dreams
convinced of their significance?
Tell all, go on, keep nothing hidden—
of course we'll listen.
Imagine an island then, a desert
of the mind, no release, no escape—
go to sleep, go back to your special place.

Obedient to domestic dictates—
rise and shine.
Open the blinds, let the light
wash clean the night's delusions.
Outside, a blue sky giving way
to clouds, a wattlebird
flashing past. Then another.
Over the road, the new neighbour
polishing his ute, three magpies
exploring the median strip.
On the fence-rail, by the gate,
a green can of VB its own mystery.

And so, meeting again, as we do
this morning, by dubious means:
mortar and pestle, a postcard
of Paris pinned to the wall—
each an article, in itself, of a faith
untested, a desire that grows unsown.
If a message was floated in a bottle
what might it say?
That the eucalypt on the traffic island
is flowering with abandon;
that bats have come for the summertime—
by May they'll be gone.
And there is nothing else like this—
nothing at all.

REQUESTED

The bath opens a blue glass page—
all night we drift, gazing at hard water,
splinters of light,
the moon its own decoration.

In this swimsuit season
skin fashions an easy audience,
teasing out the noise of men.

Mark the hours, record
the performance:
it is too late to ask questions—
breathe, patiently, into the body,
the hot stone. Sleep in it.

JOHN MATEER

ODE

Kangaroo-paw,
scarlet dipstick measuring
the depth of blood in which we live,
Bloom like one of those small
marsupial limbs appearing
redundant, shrunken
like the head of an enemy,
and yet like a rabbit's foot, an amulet –
These resemblances in a skull's museum are
not recognition, are the oxygenated
blood of living memories.

SPLITTER FALLS, LORNE

This footpath flowing along the ledge
raises me against the cliff face
over a gorge whose
rapids aren't seen behind the trees.
Morning clear with the qualia
of foliage, the unreflecting white waters
that chug like blood past shut ears.
Across from here, across the deep gash
abraded by the invisible river
a thin tributary is gushing,
splattering flat black rocks
to coalesce with the wrong gravity.
From oceanic mouths rivers should stream
back to thunderheads; mountains should
again be granular, and cold planets gas.
We should see that and be cautious, silence.
On this gorge's other side
cumulus gums sough. Spotting them,
I'm mossy, inhaling consciously.
Those white birds gliding there, sulphur-crested
cockatoos, are the pit of my stomach in lift-off.
Then they perch. They're airborne
again, then perch. Like pebbles trying to
bed down in the river, like giant cycads
tensioning a spider's thread. Under
decaying leaves, bark, wood
and aspirating soil we are already extinct.
No need to widen eyes or wait.
Every step's a rock pool, then a waterfall.
This well-worn path pulls my feet along.

THOSE IMMIGRANTS

See those rainbow lorikeets
crisscrossing the sky quick-as-a-wink?
they're second or third generation
Queensland immigrants. Now they
behave like locals: they're up at Middle
Swan in the morning, feasting
in the orchards; over Kings Park and
my head in the arvo; and, at
this time of year, this evening
they'll be down at Cottesloe
in the Norfolk pines, roaring
like a bushfire-sunset
but invisible to us.

ONE YEAR

In the summer when every terrace house seemed to welcome escaped refugees,
while the War Against Terror was being fought in my name
        in the mountains of Afganistan,

I wandered the night streets under the eyes
      of quartz-white Anzacs and invisible neurotic possums,
I haunted the suburbs, driving through industrial estates,
      waiting inside 24hour supermarkets

for the voice in my head to cease prattling in Afrikaans,
      for me to stop being a lauftmensch
and start being a citizen unafraid of the silence that sews twitching lips shut.

Nightly the police helicopter flew overhead,
      its spotlight hunting car thieves not asylum-seekers,
while in my flat I watched the vase of yellow tulips,
      their Dutch clarity unmaking this age

– We are as permanent as the Statues of Bamiyan until they were exploded;
We, the frantic, are still in Manhattan's flaming, collapsing Twin Towers,

   deciding whether to run down the stairs or up.

In the autumn, when the elms refused to shed their leaves
   and I spent the long calm days lounging at the pool,
I found myself explaining nightly to my students that simply being awake
               is not insomnia: "It's political."

THE LONG MAN OF WILMINGTON

for Brian Blanchflower

In Albany's night sky I saw it: the depth
of black stars, pores in a transparent face.

We could have been on a green, almost
invisible knoll. The Long Man of Wilmington,
chalk tracks flickering gracefully

on the facing scarp, walking as though
rising, striding, weakly flashing attention-

inattention, knocking through constellations.
He had said: "That's exactly what I felt,
that you were him, you were the hill." Whale-rocks

sank under the exhaling tide of gusty shrubs,
a ghost dolphin was released on dark sparkling
that's neither chewy blood nor Memory's black.

(For me there remains a human-sized space.)

KATE
MIDDLETON

THE QUEEN'S OCEAN

Aqua—aquamarine—sea green—
colour names she heard applied
to the waters she had never seen,

would never see. The world was stripped
from her upon stepping into France, then
recreated in her hands. A garden and

its still canals curled through her own *hameau.*
Opulent, then simple, then become
the Widow Capet, in strange enclosure

her imagination roved beyond
the cell, beyond the *Conciergerie*, tiptoed
slipshod up to the waves

she could not quite picture—at Calais,
at Le Havre, at Brest, at Point-de-Grave—
and finally beyond. She never saw the ocean.

Remember the day the news arrived at Court?
Cook, the voyager, gone. The sudden salt tears
her appropriate brine, shed for hours

spent pondering the globe a mere queen
could not traverse. Grief
lagged, nipped at his far-off corpse

a full year later, when the report came through,
and lingered later still as she pulled the volume
of his explorations closer in her tower.

Now known only by number,
Prisoner 250 let the familiar words once more
swim before her eyes—

> *In the PM*
> *hoisted out the Pinnace*
> *and Yawl in order*
>
> *to attempt a landing*
> *but the Pinnace*
> *took in water so fast . . .*

All that water! So much that,
unlike that pooling at Versailles,
at last it appeared to be *sea green*.

All that water.
Another world, an Oceania. All
that water, and her fate, risen above the tower.

COLORADO RIVER PRAYER

River
Prayer

Bless her for her wreckage and wrack

    for her tree rafts,

    for her makeshift riprap
        that gathers, sits, and splits apart again

Bless her for her boulders and river rocks—

    for the collections of stone
        forming each rapid,

    for the plungepools hidden beneath
        each cascade, each drop

and bless her for her fingerlings of silt,

    for the alluvial cargo she carries,
        spilling at last into desert

    for the sedges that hug her high waterline, creep
        green against redrock walls

    for the sandstone that feeds her hunger

    for her cattails and rushes

Bless her for her smallfry—

    for the humpback chub
        whose bulbous spine vanishes into slack face,
        who loves the turbid waters

for his bonytailed chub-cousin,
        still tramping the backwater routes
          before they flood,
          before they stagnate

for the razorback sucker
        who relishes the current's nickpoint

and for the river's pikeminnow,
        the old Colorado squawfish,

        diminished in body,
        shrunken from fishermen's tales,
          six feet long in legend
          now just this handful of flesh

And bless her for her secret, dying pockets,
      laced with salt,
        oxidised and algal-bloomed,

Bless her for her stash of desert pupfish

      for those left that cling to the brackish pools
that dot the vanished delta

YOUR FEET / LOVE POEM

Your undressed feet tell the story of my heart:
the lines troughs I could dip my hands into
to quench myself; the roughness of the nails,
dirty, and slightly squared, my roughness.

She was his model and his lover
(though I am unsure which role came first)
and from him she learned the trick of it—
later photographing the feet most revealingly.

My life is told in their naked surface.
So rarely bare they become for an instant the one
true thing: like an individually carved button,
the most sour lemon, the unbalancing abstention

of your hand. This photograph
was the most personal—no face, the identity
told in skin knotted by work, and the simplicity
of sandals. There is nothing dainty in them.

Just like there is nothing dainty in your feet.
They are browner than mine could ever be
from time spent north. A beautiful code—the language
of everything I'll never know of you.

You have touched my own feet before, with hands
infinitely warmer, in the morning as we took flight
out of winter. Your hands rested on them
and later on my belly, a lover's fingers

laced into fear. My muteness a protestation
not of the way you thought my stomach smooth
but of the difference between us. How can I say it?
Your feet, bare with nothing like the relish

of my own. Your feet. Which I have never held.

LAST POEM

I went to pick a rose for you
and found there were no roses—no *Symphony*, no *Cherish*.
     The seasons are lost in a brushstroke now,
the blankness of my inattention. And I wanted to give you
those easily crushable petals (they are so easy
                    to grieve for) but the morning frosts
have seized us all. Instead I gave you the tissue
of my thin words, and said
                    I wish these were roses.
Brought like Josephine rushed roses through the blockades,
the giddiness of bringing those buds into a new country.
          The gentle, pressable flesh of them
an explanation for my warring self. We sat together
in the cold house, the words between us withering,
               having lost the libraries of eloquence
they used to hold, the pattern of sunshine dropping through
the red lace shawl hung suspended in the window.

ESTHER

OTTAWAY

OCEAN NOCTURNE

A vinegar sky, the moon with its mouth full of cloud.
My words arrive in a squall of leaves, my silences
knotted as dragnets. You gather them up like a prophet,

trusting the eyes of your hands with these difficult signs.
How to keep faith in love's instinct, the senses translating
the tangled regrets of a lover, the tongue sharp as flax?

Our bed is a refugee raft on a black heart of water.
The surge of your body shuts out the mute moon
and its questions, your shadow is sedative.
I take you in, on an ocean deep as need.

LIMINAL LOVE SONGS

*There are three things that have proved too wonderful for me,
and four that I have not come to know: the way of an eagle in
the heavens, the way of a serpent on a rock, the way of a ship
in the heart of the sea and the way of an able-bodied man with
a maiden.*

Proverbs 30:18, 19

The way of an eagle in the heavens

Reflected in an eye, the dizzy paisley
of earth laid out for miles, the fiction
of early warning. Tallest bluff,
wind-chill written in the hunch of trees.

I cling to rock, stare at the arc
of wingspan longer than my body,
clutch at the theory of a home always
in this nest, this lover. *Time*

and unforeseen occurrence. Eggs
blotched like a hunter's moon. We kiss,
draw barbs and hooks to smoothness,
fit closer than feather. How long

can this slow pattern – caring,
paining, forgiving – take flight
and return? I trace the cliff
of your brow with my finger,

your temple's shallow chalice
the shape of a stick-raft nest
of exposure, the drop-edge
of cheekbone, imagine waking

beside you on the tallest
cliff, to the shock of height
and a hooked tongue, unable to tell you
I'm sorry. Below us, everything.

The way of a serpent on a rock

Come on then, sweet-skinned creature –
love's not one of the human rights
but something one learns

in the intricate sting
of shedding, addiction to skin
and pattern, each scale mirroring

the contour of its mate,
half-hidden, half-exposed, the memory
of my hair coming down in a certain light

coiled into the pocket of your heart.
Or instinct, the draw of sun-hot granite
to the slow belly, urge to roll back

the clenching cold; my hands
in a nest of questions. I cannot
grasp what makes a predator,

divide love from craving when we find
each other in the reptilian dark
of our separate selves,

eyes full of scales,
blood racing with sinuous hunger
to bite, to be swallowed whole.

The way of a ship in the heart of the sea

Hatchway of a vessel, the shower door
shudders on its runner, takes us inside,

I face you under the hot hiss of water, skin
plumping like soaked fruit, exhaling

like leaves, wonder where in this water
we meet, what things your skin

might breathe to mine, what things are
washed away, and whether I could name

what familiarity erodes, or whether
these points of reference –

breakers of foam on your razor,
smooth river-stones of your shoulders,

shining whalebone of your hip – have slipped into
unconscious seas, and my skin is the fish

which no longer feels the waves, my senses
are faithless as sand, and this is why

I scribble charts of you, haul in shoals
of your words, sketch the precise drape

of sheet when you sleep, why my fingers
log the swell of a blue-soft vein, why,

when you tell me you love me
I sing to myself in the roiling dark:

I am in the heart of the sea
I am in the heart.

The way of an able-bodied man with a maiden

You pluck a poinciana, walk me through humid rain
around your childhood block. Thank you,

you say, for coming here, and the flame tree's bloom
is a blood-rush to my cheek. I can't explain

why fertile chance delivered you to me,
why until this journey I have not acknowledged

your uprooting. In every story you are alone.
I tuck the flower behind my ear, stoop

to a kangaroo paw's black fist, send seeds
rattling like departing trains: clumsy on your trail

I make a mess of spoor, and can't tell
what it is that I have broken underfoot,

how to tread down the past. At the lawn's edge,
locked out of your home, you are as weary

as a man grown used to desert. I cling
to your hand, don't have the words you need.

In the hotel I stroke the petals' bruises,
mesmeric as wounds. Beneath the sheet

your hands   are the flower
        a displaced heart, aflame
you track me   seed me   tell me you will never
            go away

DIMENSION AND LIGHT

Look twice. She and I are crafty edges
butted together in Escher's lithography. Descend these stairs
with caution – two dimensions pop to three,

you're outside the square, tipped out
of your own careful drawing, as two cells
burst into that four-chambered, quicksilver heart.

Our heads are opposing poles,
two points of a compass
aiming, priming, one to earth, one to sky.

Her walls and ceiling are my viscera –
we share the vibrations of an eardrum,
music, traffic, loved voices, but only she

hears that interior percussion, my pumps and bellows,
acoustics of my secret engineering.
Since I will never hear them, perhaps these sounds

were never mine, built for her, osmotic rhythms
of blood and water, memories older than mind.
We are spoonerisms: the elements she thieves

from my bones and blood and breath
become her kidneys, fingers, tongue. We are tricks
of dimension and light. Look now, she distends

my vertical, rendering me convex
through a looking-glass of water. Witness this –
it is never the eye that is tricked,

always the brain. Her weight is magnetism.
Her elbow's point wheels across my belly's sky –
an inverse sun, a telic compass needle.

CLAIRE
POTTER

EURYDICE'S CELLAR

In a cellar where
water pipes dripped with wine
I bought a black lace
dress that had a wide
velvet bow

I thought to wear it to a friend's honorary
dinner, thought it would
please his swivel eye
the one Larkin
poeticised in a poem
about photographs
of some girl he wanted to squeeze

But we are long since
friends, and your dinner
came & went, and like
Jean Rhys who wrote
of pink underclothes she folded
back into their box
my poem hums

in similitude

Only now that I've died
and gone too far
I'll squeeze into the flimsy grey
skin of Larkin's photograph

——I'll turn the heat
up at that honorary dinner
swivelling an underworld accordion
in my eye

A WHILE

something says
a while
wait
now   then
until
bats

three thousand
have blackened your fingers
and strings of sigh
are no longer enough…………
……. when is anything ever
enough? no   is surely not
enough

go,   wade
backwards   across the planks
and arrive at the same coastline   tired, dripping
wings broken   feathers hanging   no Groucho that day in January
but then smoke cleared   and—   yellow Yellow—
nail a kiss above my door!

under a tender cloak you walk and dead leaves tremble   we eat
but somewhere else   you are whistling   skinning fish below a jetty
wondering why it is that they don't swim   anymore

unbroken
between us   the language of fireflies—

a slipknot of daffodils caught in a tide
of felty darkness

but what I mean to say is
love
doesn't need
bait   (or the preface of sticks & bone)

it needs
a line.

LADIES OF THE CANON

Far from where antique cycads sleep
I wonder about nests in a circular park
wonder how the downy baskets creep
through vines and weedy bulrushes
wonder how a nest might float
carrying five speckled pledges under midnight's coat
wonder how a bird might cheat
and drink its music from the canon

Should I unravel a nest so sweet
and arrive inside Eve's garden with its apple trees
an old Joseph-coat tugged around her shoulders
and bright bouquets standing in her eyes
in her eyes bright bouquets reflecting
Marguerite Yourcenar passing by
on oriental tales and a swallow's high
introducing me to Bessie & Patti Smith
sitting down to a table of vine and leaf
wiping chalky mouths on golden skirts
ladies of the canon tethering out their verse

A filigree table of vine and leaf
shaded by the frayed wings of old cycad trees
a stone hand pours water on the canon
which sings songs to men who've lost the confidence of birds
birds who've lost confidence in men
sing songs of regret and melancholy
weave colourful nets of seed and silk
for Eve and ladies of the canon

Wonder how a bird
might cheat and drink its music from the canon

MERMAIDS IN THE BASEMENT

I found her out there
On a slope few see,
That falls westwardly
To the salt-edged air
                    Thomas Hardy,
            'I Found Her Out There'

Having become too vociferous
even for the bathroom – in plain
morning light, long before breakfast
but after a cup of tea – he
moved his three mermaids
to the basement. The longest
led the way – disassembled herself
of hair pins, celluloid combs,
encrusted seaweed shawls, weights, coins.

She shuffled single-file
across the weft of rosebush
carpet trying to accustom
her hypothetical eyes
to the lonesome feather
caught between the cat's
sleeping paw.

In the kitchen –
in addition, he
taped garbage bags
to the linoleum – slung
a pitcher of honeyed water
and wedged doors with
soap-stones he found

discarded in a quarry – had Emily
Dickinson kept mermaids? Not necessarily
the picture-book type –
but mermaids from Neptune – ones
acclimatised to the polis. But he –
he hardly lived in a metropolis –
and Dickinson barely
left her room
but she did stitch spines
of unpublished fascicles – wrote to a Master
whom nobody knew,
chiselled his manhood
into a calligraphic noblessse
by asking the question: 'How
would you like to be *Somebody*?

However – the mermaids
have lost interest –
he promises them baths
of rose-water and brine –
offers them custody
of the gramophone horn –
its mammoth ebony shell
folding waves and sea static
– a trellis of plosive notes,
cool wing flappings, pink
and white
carousel candy, humming in the conic
of its incantatory ear.

Into the basement he
sluiced tap water equivalent
to the volume of an islet –
emptied barrels
of salt-edged braids mosaically
down the stairs. He
regarded the procession
of his absinth-coloured ghosts
as if through heat waves
as if enchanted brooms were sweeping
the last bees from
the cells of his memory-hives.

And unfolded
from his pocket
a hand-stitched envelope
that he held
without breathing
to the rift of his mouth –
knowing that its contents
and the mermaids
in the basement –
conferred the silence
of his being nobody –
with the *rat-a-tat-tat*
of his feeling
– like Somebody.

DAVID
PRATER

SUNBATHING

will only say that your hint re sunbaths
has saved me many a day's illness
                    Bernard O'Dowd
        writing to Walt Whitman (1890)

i shall take sunbaths & eat stone fruit from the goulburn valley
        reading your lines again my beloved my only one my sun for you
i shall compose letters lines verses song cycles people will eat
        oranges & know that you & i are one oh my mouth full of pips
i shall spit out words & watch them there in the grass speckled
        & wet & the galahs will circle above us wheeling & shrieking all
through the evening's long denouement pray they can hear us in
        our nests of wisdom squawking in our new language each breath
a southerly change or a billowing tent of dust in cathedrals we
        shall linger together preach at the coat-tails of strangers bellow
at believers & those they call 'godless' in glades of deception –
        for ours is a new world master a world composed of grass not
based on colour unless it be the colour of reeds & blood stilled
        in veins or that of sand in glass or the wind through rushes & if
death has a colour let us eradicate it from our rainbow we shall
        make new sounds spoken by leaves that people can actually read

OZ

final oceanic junk channel-deepened
       by temporal bo'sun of the universe

are you some castaway floating sea
       kelp island where dawning abendland

in elysian fields of restfulness recon-
       structs her deadly breeding grounds?

or are you one of the gods sun ra
       maybe following the comet kohoutek?

are you in favour of daylight savings
       bonsai maintenance massive oil wars

or just some mosquitoes flying through
       the dredged & dying murray wetlands?

could you be an untapped source
       of poisons for travelling parasites

or are you still hiding that sneaky Y2K
       virus in your unpopped pimples?

see the ANZAC memorials to the rest
       of the earth's extinct flora & fauna

that within your vast circumference
       kick against the pricks & crash down

or else act like cruel coat hangers
       & behead those riding underneath trees

blending superstition with the brave
　　　　recommendations of commissioners

to brand that theoretical spot in our
　　　　atmosphere with an unequivocal X –

where innocent & pacified collaborators
　　　　still coax those flies into your mouth

LADY LAND

to be honest with you i'm not prepared to
provide references she says (no not at this
stage well i mean you haven't been model
tenants exactly have you (rents always late
often in the shape of leaves poems & trees
i don't need if it gets paid at all (we're still
trying to reconcile the accounts as i speak
then there was the sunday gambling & the
subletting which led to all kinds of fights &
commotions on stairways & in back lanes (
& complications arising from civil claims –
as you can well imagine (in the end we had
to go to the tribunal to have you evicted &
the lock changed although what good that's
done i'm not sure . . . shipping our problems
elsewhere, hmm? hence your call i suppose
well (as i hope you'll understand we've been
swamped with all kinds of requests of late
so you should receive our reply by january
but then there's liberation day & the parade
still it's nice to know

      i remain

        yours, etc.

LURKER

i know where you're from & why you're here
doing your 'research', just 'keeping tabs' etc.
my stats reveal your browsing habits & what
brought you here, five seconds ago – cached
like a memory of some long ago private party
you never attended but heard about later (as
if that were proof enough, as if talking about
life makes it real, makes the gulf between us
seem serene as an ice-skater dragging blades
down the smooth sheet's inverse blackboard)
with a flick & a spin you're gone again traces
of your lipstick all that's left (a little pop-up
down & where did that come from? oh & yr
bookmarked tears (pretty maids all in a row

that place where we all someday hope to die
or rot at least (our skins like autumn leaves

in solidarity with those whose fame exceeds
our own (no matter now this system lets us

obscure the vain & support the humbled the
catalogue that protects that gives each of us

some space in which to rest canonised alone
awaiting some three miracles a beatification

in that heavenly curriculum (of ars poetica,
each brailled punchcard returned by hand to

its vacuum-sealed drawer (the airs condition
interpret you (guard against that lonely dew

NICK

RIEMER

THE BIRD, THE YEAR

The bird is planted on the bark, a scalloped shell,
and the tree sails on through the year. Time
and the lapping butterfly lap at the shores of the afternoon,
winter refuses. We observe the bird from every possible angle:
it is half a bird, half the ocean licking on a scalp of sand.
Now it is a second bird. (Houses fight the horizon,
a fringe of trees.) Yes, there's something about sleep,
the eyes crushing sleep into the face – the bird
now sleeping, dreaming its licey voice blaming,
drilling, the night.

That was the whole of the flower, the spring: no fish waking
in the pond, just the packet marked 'Windybank's Squid',
the long sound waves make, breaking on the shore.
The bird repeats throughout the day, a mirror
in which everything is turned: the pond a kind of bark,
the fish a kind of tree, each brick a kind
of building. That street, on which a scene
was set, has a corner no foot can see around, with traffic
like the sound of wind. In this kind of shell, the year.

PARK ANDRÉ CITROËN IN WINTER

Some things get less abstract the more you look at them.
People, for instance: those rollerblading figures moving too fast
   in the bright distance, their jointed attitudes,
black glasses hiding faces, the children's mouths
full of sentences, their different coloured coats.
      Bodies radiate shells of heat
        warped and ripped by the wind, everyone
has their own idea of what is warmth,
and the breath is snatched up before it's left your mouth,
      unlike on stiller days it rests beside you in the air,
         doing nothing.

All the usual characters, moved as though on rails.
The park is a platform, the park is like a platform on which
      everything is set, a blank between the buildings,
       each part its own obsession,
listed by the balconies of cloud. Gusts swing a fountain
      like the hands of a drunken clock,
channelled runs of water are chased by wind, throw right angles,
      reflect structures, empty sky where there cannot be sky.
On the left, garbled buildings, a heap of roofs and windows;
      the single building on the right clear, a plain glass wall.

'One, two, three, Sun.' In the distance a concrete cloud grows
      and bubbles, moulding the air.
A thin cupped hand, the bridge cradles a train.
A kid is shouting all this noise blown away to somewhere else.
The scene is holed on one side, drains into the eye of the man in
   the park.

THE MEANING PLAIN: 40 AERIAL SHOTS

1   The tops of things get closer, only the tops.
2   The Indonesian marching band marches through the Singaporean
    marching band, never touching.
3   Why does the spider monkey cross itself? Does everything always
    seem so simple?
4   A tiny scrap catches on the footpath. Stop, start, stop, start.
5   Battling a butter-thick wind on a pink bike, you're riding uphill
    through the desert.
6   The primordial wilderness: developer's dream! – the landmass fills
    with resorts.
7   I cannot be casual, I cannot be causal: indulge this Sombre, Linear
    Rhetoric.
8   A surfer with a rat's tail scans the sea through narrowed, piggy eyes,
    willing tidal waves.
9   The orchestra strikes up a seafaring crescendo.
10 There. Now I've married these words. They can never leave each
    other.
11 The couldn't-care-less Picasso mouthing: 'He paints as if he had
    swallowed the sun'.
12 On the harbour, the Opera House's bloom. White means no less than
    green.
13 The head breaks off a cherished doll.
14 The leads lie limp all over the floor.
15 What's all this 'we' business anyway? It could have been different.
16 Somewhere there's a field, and a hangar in the field
17 Full of primary colours and crumpled aircraft metal.
18 What's the point? A train ticket's full of it. You know what you
    already want.
19 The Garbage God. The God of the Here and Now. The oldest God.
20 Suddenly all the phones in a suburb, starting ringing.
21 Someone alone in a landscape far too often, wallowing in reality.

22 Looking down the shiny corridor, carriage on carriage on carriage.
    A sad and guilty vandal loops designs.
23 By the recycling bins: a shevelled woman asks for money.
24 They're not sad! They're stoked, ecstatic! (In writing, I protest,
    there's no white paint).
25 Slow-motion, dimly seen: caked in mud, the dead GIs peel themselves
    off the jungle floor, their movements perfectly synchronised.
26 A small crowd has gathered under the cliffs of her silence.
27 Through the streets will we walk, spotting the Mouths of Truth, the
    Fried-Egg Plant.
28 The wind over Long Bay, reallocating pressure. 'Psychiatric' prisoners
    feel their bodies fill with medicine.
29 Over to the Aztecs, sitting round in the past, playing with paper,
    torturing each other.
30 The knife and fork of the Holy Spirit. That's it.
31 What's the connection between truth and pain, the advertiser wonders.
32 We have landed in the cloudless Western Suburbs of the world. Our
    choices are petty, ignorant: others are to blame as well.
33 A snap-fit model of the Space Shuttle lying half assembled on the
    workshop bench.
34 The cabin crew smirk, serve orange juice again.
35 A self-contained person, the farmer. Clears blackberry in the
    ringbarked light. His battered checked shirt, top few buttons undone.
    Statuesque, but his shoulder is aching.
36 A shadow curves where light has set on white unpainted plastic.
37 The Patriarch pauses, calculating Easter. How badly he wants a flight
    simulator on his computer.
38 Panic! Cheese everywhere – *everywhere*!!!
39 The view out this window: the city and the suburbs.
40 This poem is broken, it won't work anymore.

THE THING YOU'RE IN

Everything happens fast and then is gone –
the new movie you were waiting for
that you've suddenly just seen, the tunnel
under the harbour that seemed to take forever
now built and grooved by a million trips.
In winter fruit trees bud, shops
are full of summer clothes; only this
mind is slow, still stalling on the same
old questions, never getting it, left behind
by life as by some wild-eyed nag
storming down the street, the hoofprints
pasted in the grass.

And how little of this can actually be seen,
the past as it streaks into the distance behind you,
the tail-lights that blur and merge with the afterglow
of silent buildings? World, dirty emerald,
I accuse! You're the world and not
its photocopy, ragged-edged and tatty.

And the flower of the moment is too light
to notice, let alone pluck; you sit there on
the nose-cone of your life, buried in the sofa,
where you'll watch as all the late-night
films gradually become identical. Before
too long you'll be dead, the screen of life
will be burned right through – go ask
the water riding down the sink what it knows of
death, for this is real speed and it knows more
than me. I type a full stop and an arrow
appears: today is a flickering thing, there's
not much I could say about today.

JAYA
SAVIGE

SUMMER FIG

A serene riot of bees, a pollen air,
one by one they zero in
on the bougainvillea. Our backyard god's
a giant fig, downloading
gigs of shade onto the fresh cut grass.
Under the house, your summer dress
pegged by the shoulders
approaches and ebbs, a tidal apparition.
Pause on the back steps, Mona Lisa tea-
towel flung over your shoulder, and watch
your laundry wade out on the breeze
like a family in the shallows
of a languid estuary at Mooloolah.
To not spill this thimbleful of stillness.
Soon we will return to the impossible
puzzle of light, cut by hot
oscilloscopes. Even now the crisp
silhouette of a crow sharpens itself
upon the rusting apex of the hill's hoist,
caws, cocks for an answer. This time
we let it ring out, a black cell
buzzing across the dresser
when we are both undressed.

DRANSFIELD IN BAVARIA

In the high land of the swan
autumn burns a path to Neuschwanstein,
castle of the mad king who had stars
cut into his bedroom ceiling, then
lit them with candles to soothe him
when he woke from bad dreams.

Blackbirds are speaking German techno
again, trilling glitches. Our eskimo
friend spills his gluhwein on the snow:

wildberry birthmark, blood-red Rorschach,
enough to suspect a discarded carcass
nearby, an eviscerated swan: *fox news*.

Pan's stone flute glued with ice.
Munich's cold slap shocked us

exiting the Hauptbahnhof. Now
we photograph the frozen fountain,

flicking to macro to capture the sun
jinxing the ice in beads of focus.

All-you-can-eat sushi surprised us
over the Starnbergersee. We digest
in the cemetery. Wintry pneumatics:

air hisses as you untwist a sprite.
Cue the mechanised hedgehogs
and lambs of the shopfront nativity.

On the train from Gmund, you look up
from your book at acres of crisp snow

and think of the man whose Beethoven
ringtone interrupted the guide's explanation
that morning at Small Fortress, Terezin.

The children cry *Tannenbaum! Tannenbaum!*

To quit heroin you have to leave the country,
the novelist says with a wink.

I wonder what you would have made
of Europe. What I'd have made of junk.

I guess I've never truly understood
the romance of those ruins of the blood.

THE PAIN SWITCH

The moon's white knife, etching its cold
signature in your skin, strikes bone.
Butoh shapes snap across the ruin
of your face, taut as a top sheet in a ward.
The pain switch is useless, morphine enough
to kill a horse bucked off. As am I,
awake at the foot of your bed, listening
to your c fibres fire, packets of fascist
electrochemical mail stitching up
your body's free speech each split second.
I've become devout, pray each time
the coming dark snags in your throat.
Sunlight smirks through the curtain
when the nurse shakes my wrist,
saying *It's time.* I grasp your hand,
realise you've been holding on for this.
Your vanquished sigh, a sharp, hot fist.

LA QUERCIA DEL TASSO

Here, take my weight, for I am light as shadow
since the lightning. Iron-corset,
air-conditioner, satellite dish, the rooftops sing
to me above the eternal city.

Prop me up under my armpits, please.
Help me reach the cookie-moon, the furthest shelf,
and I will sing for you.
Rust with me awhile, little tourist,
together we'll become the one misshapen thing,
gnarled with winter. Marry me
and I'll ensure we suffer no imposters: a few initials,
some condom packets, an empty bottle of Fosters,
                    so that no guest
will ever guess a poet took
his lunch here once, breathing crumbs
       of sun. Breathe on my behalf until
the burning starts. The time will come
when I will need to breathe for you, when we two
will crackle, our cinders' unobserved
parabolas like brief, celestial monsters, or space-
            junk some call shooting stars.

MARIA

TAKOLANDER

TABLEAUX

for Charlie Quarrell

I might have imagined the crabs;
      the mud came alive and subsided so quickly.
      You missed it, child-slow,

and the strange forms life takes to live are yet for you
      the stuff of animation and comedy.
      You laugh sideways at my story about these grave crawlers

as if you could see Daffy's beak spinning on his pin-head or
      Coyote reduced, split-second, to an ashen silhouette.
      Perhaps one day I'll tell you

about the seals on a desert coast in Namibia,
      dragging themselves across sand-stretches and wave-crashed rocks
      like swarms of amputees,

while in the hazy distance
      sloped the panting shapes of hyenas.
      Then there were the baboons in South Africa,

hunched quietly in the windblown sand hills above
      the ancient clash of the Atlantic and Pacific,
      their fur moving like grass,

while on the violent shoreline penguins teemed like babies.
      With your soft hand in mine we move
      over the pocked mudflats of the Tooradin foreshore.

Jellyfish drift in the murky water like ghosts,
      and further down the tideless beach, pelicans,
      with their newborn or ancient skulls,

stand before an audience of cormorants and gulls,
>   ankle deep in mud.
>   One night in Zambia I saw

a tree full of vultures, spot-lit.
>   They were hulking like souls,
>   and it was as if the world itself had died there.

Will I ever tell you that?
>   The stranded mangroves stink like a rare sea,
>   and suddenly you let go, running

towards the boat ramp and the floating jetty.
>   The sky, low-grey, accepts the motley outrage
>   of the birds without ado.

CANASTA FOR LOVERS

Hold the hearts close to your heart:
they will feed each other blooms of colour

and the nudity of shapes
until you are bursting

with the need to hold it all in.
For you must never call a spade a spade:

your lover is angular, a dark, cemetery stranger.
Look at your lover that way.

Diamonds, the distraction of arithmetic,
can be anyone's friend.

Clubs are for striking.
When you foresee the end,

get out before your lover does.
Enjoy the orgasm of discarding.

Endure the afterglow
of solitude and spite.

ANAESTHETIC

for David McCooey

       Valium-nice, this business of death,
this chemical smile

       that floats my body, bundled in snow and hay,
above a hospital tray,

       where flesh and time take wing like sin,
and I become

       this white light and space,
pure, nothing.

       Is this what they waited for,
those god-heavy trolls,

       with their big hands and brown eyes,
as they crouched

       with their mercury liquor under dank stone bridges,
year after year,

       in summer grass and winter sludge, until they
drowned themselves there:

       my great uncle, whose leg was shot off among
the mottled birch

       where Soviet tanks and silent Finnish gunmen played at chess
in the snow;

my youngest uncle, who stole from his old mother to slake
his darkling thirst;

and my eldest cousin, who died only months ago, leaving
a drunken ex-wife and a son with myopia?

Is this what I wanted during those leaden times,
when with every mouthful

I swallowed the burning world, offering myself to
the execution and release

of an earth-bound history, and is it
what I am given now

only because I am godless (except for you)
and happy?

Meanwhile, Egyptian morticians manage my corpse
for resurrection.

I wake to the human condition
—mine anyway—

heavy as a hangover, but faithful to the miracles
of science,

so much kinder than religion, and to your imminent
and hallowed coming.

UNBORN

for Samuel Takolander

1. Morning sickness

I had lost myself in a novel by Marie Darrieussecq
in which a woman grows bacon skin—broken by
hair that claws with its roots, coarser than on her
pudenda—and teats like gelatinous melanomas.
I saw her fretting and muddying the earth until her
rear end let forth a litter of mutant-lets, pink and
coarse as tongues and slippery. Their lids were serene
as if eyes did not exist, and their ears were closed
to the sound of their own not screaming. It was then
I felt the tide come in, bearing silt stirred from the
fetid sea floor, old with starfish and eel bones. The
moon, for nine months, did not care to claim it again.

2. Ultrasound

I had read that some women feed life with scratched
hunks of earth that gravel their teeth, with the residue
of fire that sludges their gums, and with the odourless
powder their grandmothers used to stiffen petticoats
of crinoline. I imagine the starch creaming my throat grey,
and to us you look colourless as if you were made that way.
Still emerging from yourself, the bud of your nose alone
makes the universe less impossible. You do not know
that we are here, but this is how we watch you: on a
black-and-white plasma screen suspended on a wall
—the happy technician flicking us between dimensions
like Dr Who—and as if from an infinite distance.

3. Foetal movement

In my guidebook to pregnancy, a pencil illustration offers me
a profile of myself: armless and headless, legs to mid-thigh,
only my reproductive organs and waste channels sketched in.
My abdomen encases an upside-down foetus above the
bulbous and textured outline of my rectal cavity, the muscular,
smudged passage of my vagina and my clear urinary tract.
The caption announces that by the end of the seventh month
the foetus can respond to taste, light and sound, and it can cry.
As I watch you shadow box with sourness, radiance and din,
the sources of which you must fear like a medieval Christian,
you make of my belly a theatre for unseen marionettes and
for pain that has no origin—except for the life I have given.

47 DEGREES

re: Black Saturday

Like succulents and the nocturnal,
my newborn and I keep secrets from the sun.

He consents to being lulled by the air conditioner
in the absence of my heart and lungs.

While we sleep, cots are x-rayed into molten,
and radiance seals the eyes of women and men.

Black-out. Torchlight in my child's room
catches his silent, cloth-bound watching.

The world, at dawn, is a tray for yesterday's cigarettes,
unattended for my infant and his lush bawling.

SAMUEL WAGAN WATSON

FLOODLIGHT SONATAS

white spark backdrop
off the forms seduced by blackness,

I hate travelling at night

unable to stomach the singing of the lonely road
or the whispers
of a deadman's mouth harp in the breeze

bringing on premonitions of sudden engine failure

and,
how the halogen lamps ruin the night
and sometimes expose the
memories you're running from

I see the faces
I dare not speak of in focus
as my ritual humming of nursery rhymes
keeps in time with a pounding in my chest
desperate, until I reach my destination,
that the hairy hands in the back seat
won't materialise from my
retrospective sins
and take a deserved piece of me

or merely,
        just a taste

JETTY NIGHTS

it was an arm that stretched over the mud and sharks
from under the song of the swaying pines in the darkness,
the night water fondles the pylons
as mullet dance in the cold blackness afraid of nothing
we too, walk against our curfew
we see the eyes under the jetty,
phosphorescence and ectoplasm
under the death of the floorboards
looking up from the muddy grave
stealing a glance at the clear cover of stars

a fishing boat drones somewhere out there on the water
and in the distance a buoy flashes red lights and green
and you suddenly feel the loneliness out there
that's where you can escape to

the smell of mashed potatoes and chops hang in the air
drags our attention back to the shoreline cottages
Ray Martin chatters somewhere in the glow of sixty watt lighting

we turn and face the clatter of dead wood
our lifeline home
and leave our jetty,
leave away the mystical squawks of curlew in the swamp
that eerie bleakness we came to love,
this innocence we behold
that we had nothing to fear but our parents' scorn

BONE YARD, SOUTH BRISBANE

the swings in the Musgrave Park night
rattle a morose and deserted song
throwing their voices
                silhouettes across an abandoned canvas

a jungle-gym resembles the half sunken remains
of a prehistoric beast
ribcage reaching for the moonlight
or an arthritic fist
                  frozen in protest

the stoic in this wilderness
feeding on the scraps of light
tossed down from the pedestals
                      of the city's neon gods.

REVOLVER

From my balcony I can read a strong poem that the moon has pasted on the river. Everything is quiet. Now and then, a wave breaks the message, temporarily changing the font from **bold** to *italics*. The moon in its crescent appearance is the precision blade of a Shaolin warrior. I'm concerned that if I gaze too long, I may carelessly jag my retinas on its razor points, pierced globes adding vitreous humor into this serious stretch of river. A mullet leaps from the water and reconstructs the moon's message; it is now the sound of one silver hand clapping. Above, an anonymous comet breaches the sky a small eternity, but shooting stars don't have the recoil of a poem executed in the lull of moon fire.

oval mirror lights
seduction on night-water,
flagrant moon kisses

NIGHT RACING

night racing through the suburbs
of white stucco dreaming
the menacing glow of the city's tainted body behind us
as the custodians of the estate domiciles
spy through the holes in their lace curtains
at the howl of our twin-cam war party
drowning out the dying heartbeat of this captured landscape
our small bodies shivering a *techno* pulse

hugging into corners
accelerating onto the straits
a growling junkyard dingo under the bonnet,
the beast made up from parts here and there
born for the walkabout rally
black feet pumping racing pedal to floor
breaking the silence of the settlers' sacred sites
enveloped in shadows when not haunted by the silhouettes of
        urban myth

mind navigation into the bitumen labyrinth
these areas we treat with the same contempt as laid upon us
as middle-class Australia prepares for another evening
darkness and the dreaming of jaywalkers and nightstalkers
yes, it cradles us too
like the Earth Mother did the warriors of old
but we're too scared to look behind us or in the rear-view mirror
to catch a wink from Voodoojack
                        and his perpetual black grin

SIMON
WEST

TO WAKE IN SOMEONE ELSE'S DREAM

To wake in someone else's dream.
Weather warmed bare arms
and the inner arch of feet.
In a capital of lost provinces
to keep crossing avenues of flowering *tiglio*.
Unmarked doors were just ajar,
all the birds were facing south.
Lime trees, we reminded ourselves.
Lime tea at all hours.

And somewhere a flock of pigeons rose.
No, click of slats as old women drew their blinds.
And a heckle of car horns was heard.
No, bells that summoned from a distant church.
And listen, a blackbird, now, at dawn, not evening.
'Happy as a blackbird,' you said,
talking as if at home.
Branches were dark under summer leaves,
and not a whit less solid.

VOLATILES

Strange for the season, but there it was,
a cold wind from the south. Dead or insect-
ravaged leaves were shaken off river gums
and whirled hard across a tract where the Goulburn
opened the bush like a furrow. It pulled me up,
as if a Sibyl's scattered forecasts
were there for the grabbing.
Each had turned to a hovering moment,
a way back to reckon the day's alloy
odd as a bower bird's hoard: bright trinket-words,
gut-wrenches, regrets. It was a flash of reprieve
that let you broach what otherwise
yielded to the need to carry on, and already,
like these volatiles, was spiralling down
to hit the surface with a shock. Suddenly
they too had been caught and were part of the current's
impetus: just leaves again.

A MINOR SENSE

It starts with a dog barking in the distance.
Another further off. Crickets
somewhere. Traffic on the road.
Under the backyard gum
you stand stunned to have cleared
the mind a moment.
In the key of a minor sense,
an awareness of surroundings,
and through a window without curtains
a light glows in your own empty room.
You know when you take
a deep breath and can feel the air?
Well, that's how it is,
here, in place, at the end of the day.
But all this, is it told in praise?
And on what grounds?
And it's gone, as you circle in.

ANEMOGRAMS

Anemograms from years you can hardly remember
handed round at an evening garden party.
Empty envelopes the colour of envy,
sparkling wine and cautious laughter.
A guest who has waited too long
makes an awkward proposal.

Pronunciation. And longing.
Fears that seemed so large as shadows,
walking barefoot now through prickly grass.

No one anymore wears white silk gloves.
She came from Wilno and the century
of grand railway stations, and spoke many languages.
Yes, tonight there is an uncanny resemblance
to the northerlies of our childhood,
as if another time might come.

OUT OF THE WOOD OF THOUGHTS

We woke with the crook of our arms empty.
Each morning the triple-cooing turtle-dove
would probe about our yard,
'coo-ca-cai?' A nag and hullabaloo
I couldn't help but hear as 'cosa fai?'

Mostly summer turned away, tightened
to a knot of roots at river's edge,
where earth erodes from a red gum,
unable to grip things, strangely exposed.

No use saying 'it was him not me',
or 'dispel the senses and repeat, The mind lies'.
Even the faintest trails led back to that weight
cradled in the stomach's pit.
What was *it* doing? What did *it* have to say?

MARNPI ROCKHOLE
BY MICK NAMARARA TJAPALTJARRI

This is rock undone
                    to its roots,
to a level hard to see
where leptons
tug against quarks and grip sheer air
into substance.
                    To look at this is mass imagined
as it shimmers in a frenzy
of particles and bliss.

There is no sense of hurry in the map, no
x-marks-the-spot.
                    Perhaps something is
hidden in the landscape. But not to pin-point.
                    More like a
current of water or the wind's course. A careful
child might still guess at it.

Coloured lines flow across the canvas –
charcoals, ochres, white: colour
                    loosened of things until
the surface ripples like a breached pool.
Our bearings dance in a mirage
and the naked eye
can't moor.

Somewhere among shifting sandhills
there is a fold,
                    a slit where the mind's eye
grafts in dimensions that have no horizon.
This is the rockhole.
This is where it dissolves and dissolves.

PETRA

WHITE

MAGNOLIA TREE

A mind beginning to know itself again
after a long period of hostage
to itself, its germs, its own wrong slant.
No beauty, no blooms,
but ugliness of repetition,
a world like a pill of grey,
dissolving in a glass of grey.
Never to be caught and never free,
like the sea when it is by itself,
as personal as a message, and blank and nameless.
The medicated mind begins again,
tries to imagine itself, a dance
of a dance, each step a memory,
this is me, it says, *this is how I'd be*,
with a notion of I as the one true self
hard as a bud, white as a bloom
that yet goes under, that cries in the night
for mysterious help.
Lowell called it murderous,
its five-day blooming. I have moved my bed
to see it where it blooms,
on every twig the white flowers open.

KARRI FOREST

near Manjimup, Western Australia

It swirls you in its poem, slows the protester
chained to a tree, the logger chainsawing his
future together, to the pace of chessmen,
in a battle that must be waged one-tree-at-
a-time on moral ground stodgy as mud.

Sepia tangles of tree-waste, the earth
lifting its bare prickly head: what to do
with all this light – is it light? At night I walked
into the forest (what remained). Moonlight
brazened on the scabby wood, red Xs

scrawled on bark; already there, the dead tree
across my path I couldn't seem to cross,
the corpse I killed and buried and forgot,
in a dream that wakes and circles, always
convinces, as one's guilt always feels right.

NOTES FOR THE TIME BEING

How many sonnets must we write
before the great gong sounds in Heaven?
Peter Porter

Relieved like a criminal
at last apprehended
and tricked out of daylight.
Will I be you again?

Too much freedom
is not enough.
How large or small the world
where time fits.

Terrible thing a head
from which no thought escapes.
As the world said
good-bye to you

it grew small and glazy,
a thing seen beneath tears
as when a child says good-bye
to a too-much-trouble pet.

Soul frees itself
(from something),
or tries to imagine
it gone, the heavy –

still carrying
what's precious
– the gold, the old –
and the fuse hope.

Thrown into light, thrown into dark,
etc. Where does illness live,
what does it want?
And sits before the Sybil,

begging for speech.
Describe your fear.
How do you feel out of 10?
Out of 9?

Soul is confused, sad for no reason,
can't remember;
sits in her chair and stares
like someone much older
who'll never again remember.

Weeps, as if out of the corner
of humanity's loose mouth;
her tears are lost coins, spilling down
the loud spiral of that machine,
somewhere in eternity, that codes them:

Grief 1, Grief 2, and
how unusual: Griefs 11 and 19.
And sometimes, of course, there is joy,
also for no reason – here you ask
what has reason got to do with it? –

THE GONE

We turn them to stone when they go.
(It is always them and us
with the dead.)
They have mostly been dead
too long to still be mourned.
The tilting graves are exhibitions
built up inside: here are parents,
children and grandchildren,
flat-packed into the present tense *here lie*
and the single past tense of the headstone.
They have slipped beyond family
and twinkle anonymously
in the magical DNA that lies
about like powder at the edge of things.
But our own dead are everywhere.
Closing our eyes at night,
we imagine ourselves like them,
perhaps in a zone where forever
we might freeze, or a sea
or river we swim for all durations.
They tour that multiplex
of wherever-we-think-them-to-be:
shadowing us to work, leaping onto the bus,
standing by the filing cabinet, chatting.
Something about existence
insists on presence.
The dead, surely they just want life again,
and it is there:
haunting them up to their eaves,
clinging to their hands like ropes of ghost-cloth,
vexing their spoon drawers,
blitzing their screens with images.

ABOUT THE CONTRIBUTORS

Ali Alizadeh was born in Iran in 1976. He began writing in Persian prior to immigrating to Australia in 1991. His first English poem was published in his early twenties while studying creative arts at Griffith University. Ali has since published six books of poetry, fiction and creative non-fiction, the latest of which is the collection of poems *Ashes in the Air* (UQP, 2011). Ali holds a PhD in professional writing from Deakin University. He lives with his wife and son.

Louis Armand is the author of the poetry collections *Séances* (Twisted Spoon Press, 1998), *Inexorable Weather* (Arc Publications, 2001), *Land Partition* (Textbase, 2001), *Strange Attractors* (Salt Publishing, 2003), *Malice in Underland* (Textbase, 2003), *Picture Primitive* (Antigen, 2006) and *Letters from Ausland* (Vagabond Press, 2011), along with two volumes of prose fiction, *The Garden* (Salt Publishing, 2001) and *Menudo* (Antigen, 2006). He is the editor of *Contemporary Poetics* (Northwestern University Press, 2007) and author of several volumes of criticism, including *Solicitations: Essays on Criticism and Culture* (Litteraria Pragensia Books, 2005). He currently edits the magazine *VLAK: Contemporary Poetics & the Arts*.

Emily Ballou is a poet, novelist and screenwriter. Her collection *The Darwin Poems* (UWAP, 2009) was awarded the Wesley Michel Wright Prize, highly commended in the Anne Elder Award and shortlisted for the New South Wales Premier's Kenneth Slessor Prize, the Mary Gilmore Award, the Western Australian Premier's Prize and the ALS Gold Medal.

Judith Bishop (b. 1972) is a poet and professional linguist. Her first poetry collection, *Event* (Salt Publishing, 2007), won the Anne Elder

Award and was shortlisted for the Victorian Premier's CJ Dennis Prize for Poetry, the Queensland Premier's Judith Wright Calanthe Award and the Mary Gilmore Award. Her poem 'Openings' shared the Peter Porter Poetry Prize in 2010. Judith lives in Sydney with her husband and two young daughters.

Michael Brennan was born in Sydney in 1973. His first collection, *The Imageless World* (Salt Publishing, 2003), won the Mary Gilmore Award and was shortlisted for the Victorian Premier's CJ Dennis Prize for Poetry. *Unanimous Night* (Salt Publishing, 2008) won the William Baylebridge Memorial Prize and was shortlisted for the New South Wales Premier's Kenneth Slessor Prize. He has also published a collaboration titled 空は空 with Japanese installation artist Akiko Muto. His poetry has been translated into French, Japanese, Chinese and Spanish. He lives in Tokyo, where he is an associate professor in the Faculty of Policy Studies, Chuo University.

Michelle Cahill is a Goan-Anglo-Indian poet. Born in Kenya in 1969, she attended primary school in London before migrating to Australia. She lives in Sydney, where she works part-time as a GP. She was highly commended in the Blake Poetry Prize and received the Val Vallis Poetry Award in 2010 and the minor prize in the Inverawe Nature Poetry Competition. Her collections are *The Accidental Cage* (Interactive Press, 2006), a chapbook titled *Ophelia in Harlem* (Kilmog Press, 2010) and *Vishvarūpa* (Five Islands Press, 2011).

Elizabeth Campbell lives in Melbourne, where she was born in 1980. She has received the Vincent Buckley Poetry Prize and a residency for 2011 at the BR Whiting Library, Rome. She teaches English and literature at a government secondary school. Her two books of poems, *Letters to the Tremulous Hand* and *Error*, are published by John Leonard Press.

Justin Clemens writes poetry and criticism. His most recent poetry collections include *Villain* (Hunter Publishers, 2009) and *Me 'n' me Trumpet* (Vagabond Press, 2011). A book-length selection of his art criticism, entitled *Minimal Domination*, is imminent from Surpllus Press. He teaches at the University of Melbourne.

Joel Deane is a poet, novelist, speechwriter and journalist. Born in Melbourne, he grew up in regional Victoria and, aged seventeen, started out as a copyboy on a Melbourne tabloid newspaper. He spent six years in the San Francisco Bay area, returning to Australia to work for the Labor Party as a press secretary and speechwriter. He has published two novels, two collections of poetry and one chapbook. His most recent poetry collection, *Magisterium* (Australian Scholarly Publishing, 2008), was shortlisted for the Melbourne Prize for Literature Best Writing Award. Joel's most recent novel is *The Norseman's Song* (Hunter Publishers, 2010). He lives in Melbourne.

Kate Fagan is a poet, editor and songwriter whose books include *The Long Moment* (Salt Publishing, 2002), *Thought's Kilometre* (Tolling Elves, 2003) and *return to a new physics* (Vagabond Press, 2000). A new collection entitled *First Light* is forthcoming from Giramondo Publishing. Kate is a former editor of *How2* journal and is from one of Australia's pre-eminent folk music families, The Fagans. Her album *Diamond Wheel* won the National Film and Sound Archive Folk Recording Award (www.katefagan.com).

Jane Gibian's publications include her collection *Ardent* (Giramondo Publishing, 2007) and *small adjustments and other poems* (*Wagtail* poetry magazine, Picaro Press, 2008). Her work has been widely anthologised, most recently in *Motherlode: Australian Women's Poetry 1986–2008* (Puncher & Wattman, 2009) and *The Perfume River: Writing from Vietnam* (UWAP, 2010).

Lisa Gorton lives in Melbourne. Her poetry collection *Press Release* (Giramondo Publishing, 2007) was shortlisted for the Melbourne Prize for Literature Best Writing Award and the Mary Gilmore Award, and won the Victorian Premier's CJ Dennis Prize for Poetry. She studied at Melbourne University and Oxford University, where she completed a doctorate on John Donne's poetry and prose. Lisa has also written a children's novel, *Cloudland* (Pan Macmillan, 2008), and been awarded the Vincent Buckley Poetry Prize and the John Donne Society Award for Distinguished Publication in Donne studies. Her next collection, *The Hotel Hyperion*, is forthcoming from Giramondo Publishing.

Libby Hart's most recent collection of poetry, *This Floating World*, is published by Five Islands Press. Her first collection, *Fresh News from the Arctic* (Interactive Press, 2006), received the Anne Elder Award and was shortlisted for the Mary Gilmore Award. She is a recipient of an Australia Council for the Arts residency at the Tyrone Guthrie Centre at Annaghmakerrig (Ireland) and a DJ O'Hearn Memorial Fellowship at The Australian Centre (University of Melbourne). *This Floating World* was devised for stage and performed by Teresa Bell and Gavin Blatchford. These performances received the Shelton Lea Award for Best Group Performance at the 9th Melbourne Overload Poetry Festival.

Sarah Holland-Batt has lived in Australia, the United States, Italy and Japan. Her first book, *Aria* (UQP, 2008), was awarded the Arts ACT Judith Wright Prize, the Thomas Shapcott Poetry Prize, and the Anne Elder Award. As of late 2010, she is the WG Walker Memorial Fulbright Scholar at New York University.

LK Holt lives in Melbourne. Her first poetry collection, *Man Wolf Man* (John Leonard Press, 2009), won the New South Wales Premier's Kenneth Slessor Prize. Her second collection, *Patience, Mutiny* (John Leonard Press, 2010), won the Grace Leven Poetry Prize. She is co-editor of *So Long Bulletin*.

Emma Jones is from Sydney. Her first book, *The Striped World*, was published by Faber & Faber in 2009.

Danijela Kambaskovic-Sawers teaches Shakespeare and Renaissance studies at the University of Western Australia. She migrated from the former Yugoslavia in 1999, writes in two languages, reads several more, specialises in poetry and Shakeseparean translation, and considers history her playpen, aiming to infect as many people as possible with the No-Future-Without-the-Past virus. Danijela has published poetry across the former Yugoslavia and in Australia, and won the Arts ACT David Campbell Prize. *Atlantis* and *Journey*, her two books of poetry, appeared in Serbia; her third (but first Australian) collection, *Internal Monologues – A Romance*, is forthcoming from Fremantle Press.

Bronwyn Lea is the author of *Flight Animals* (UQP, 2001), the winner of the Wesley Michel Wright Prize and the Anne Elder Award, and *The Other Way Out* (Giramondo Publishing, 2008), the winner of the South Australian Premier's John Bray Poetry Award and the Western Australian Premier's Book Award for Poetry. In 2011 she was appointed the inaugural editor of *Australian Poetry Journal*.

Cameron Lowe lives in Geelong, where he was born in 1973. His two poetry collections are the chapbook *Throwing Stones at the Sun* (2005) and *Porch Music* (2010), both published by Whitmore Press. He is currently a PhD candidate in the School of Culture and Communication at the University of Melbourne.

John Mateer has published a number of books in Australia, as well as smaller publications that have appeared in South Africa, Australia, Indonesia, Japan, Macau and Portugal. Among his works are the books *Ex-white: South African Poems* (Sysphus Verlag, 2009), *The West: Australian Poems* (Fremantle Press, 2010) and *Southern Barbarians* (Giramondo Publishing, 2011). He has read his work in many countries, and in 2010 he was invited to read at PEN's Free the Word Festival in London.

David McCooey is a poet, critic, and academic. His first book of poems, *Blister Pack* (Salt Publishing, 2005), won the Mary Gilmore Award, and was shortlisted for four other major awards. His second full-length collection, *Outside*, is forthcoming from Salt Publishing. He is deputy general editor of the *Macquarie PEN Anthology of Australian Literature* (Allen & Unwin, 2009), which won a New South

Wales Premier's Literary Award. He has written widely on Australian literature, especially Australian poetry and life writing. He lives and works in Geelong, being an associate professor in literary studies and professional and creative writing at Deakin University.

Kate Middleton's first poetry collection, *Fire Season* (Giramondo Publishing, 2009), won the Western Australian Premier's Book Award for Poetry. She has completed an MFA in poetry at the University of Michigan and an MA in literature at Georgetown University.

Esther Ottaway's poetry has been published widely, commissioned for the Sydney Writers' Festival and other festivals, featured on ABC Radio National programs, and set to music for the Tasmanian Symphony Orchestra. *Blood Universe* (Poets Union, 2006) – a collection of poems on pregnancy – attracted national acclaim, and poems from it appeared in *The Australian* and the major anthologies *Motherlode* (Puncher & Wattman, 2008) and *Swings & Roundabouts* (Random House, 2008). Esther has won the Tom Collins Poetry Prize, the Australian Young Poets' Fellowship, a Varuna residency, Arts Tasmania grants and other prizes. She lives in Hobart with her musician husband and daughter.

Felicity Plunkett has been UQP's poetry editor since 2010. She has a PhD from the University of Sydney, and is a poet and critic. Her first collection, *Vanishing Point* (UQP, 2009), won the Thomas Shapcott Poetry Prize, and was shortlisted for several other major awards. Her chapbook, *Seastrands*, was published in 2011 as part of Vagabond Press's Rare Objects series. Her essays on and reviews of Australian poetry have been widely published.

Claire Potter was born in 1975 in Perth, Western Australia. *In Front of a Comma* (Poets Union), her first chapbook, appeared in 2006 as part of an Australian Young Poets' Fellowship, and since then she has published poetry, criticism and translations. She spent five years studying and teaching in Paris, and now lives in London. *Swallow*, her first full-length collection, was published in 2010 by Five Islands Press.

David Prater was born in Dubbo, New South Wales, in 1972. He holds a BA from the University of Sydney, an MA from the University of Melbourne and a PhD from Swinburne University of Technology. His first poetry collection, *We Will Disappear*, was published by papertiger media in 2007, and Vagabond Press published his chapbook *Morgenland* in the same year. Since 2001 he has been the managing editor of *Cordite Poetry Review* (www.cordite.org.au), an online journal of Australian poetry and poetics. He currently lives in Karlskrona, Sweden, where he is undertaking post-doctoral research on electronic literature and pedagogy at Blekinge Tekniska Högskola.

Nick Riemer was born in 1972 in Sydney, a city from which he has never managed to extricate himself for any substantial period. His collection, *James Stinks (and so does Chuck)*, was the first book published by Puncher & Wattmann in 2005.

Jaya Savige was born in Sydney in 1978 and grew up on Bribie Island and in Brisbane, Queensland. His first collection, *Latecomers* (UQP, 2005), was awarded the Thomas Shapcott Poetry Prize and the New South Wales Premier's Kenneth Slessor Prize. In 2007 he was a writer in residence at the BR Whiting Library, Rome. He is currently reading for a PhD in English at the University of Cambridge. His latest collection is *Surface to Air* (UQP, 2011).

Maria Takolander is the author of a book of poems, *Ghostly Subjects* (Salt Publishing, 2009), which was shortlisted for the Queensland Premier's Judith Wright Calanthe Award. She was also winner of the inaugural *Australian Book Review* Elizabeth Jolley Short Story Prize. Her poetry, fiction and essays have been widely published. She is a senior lecturer in literary studies and creative writing at Deakin University in Geelong.

Samuel Wagan Watson is a writer of Aboriginal, German and Irish descent. Born in Brisbane in 1972, much of his work is inked from the muddy-mangrove resins of Moreton Bay where he grew up. An author of several award-winning collections of poetry, Samuel divides his time between family, writing and broadcasting, and has now found a career as the principal writer at one of Australia's premier Indigenous radio stations, 98.9FM.

Simon West is the author of *First Names* (Puncher & Wattmann, 2006) and *The Selected Poetry of Guido Cavalcanti* (Troubador, 2009). Further information can be found at www.simonwestpoetry.com.

Petra White was born in Adelaide in 1975 and now lives in Melbourne, where she works for a government department. Her first book, *The Incoming Tide* (John Leonard Press, 2007), was shortlisted in the Queensland Premier's Literary Awards and the ACT Poetry Prize; her second, *The Simplified World* (John Leonard Press, 2010), won the Grace Leven Prize.

ACKNOWLEDGMENTS

UQP would like to thank its contributors for generously offering their poems for publication in *Thirty Australian Poets*. For permission to reproduce the poems, thanks and acknowledgment are also made to the following:

Ali Alizadeh
Salt Publishing for 'I, the Monster' and 'Rumi' from *Eyes in Times of War* (2006).

'Listening to Michael Jackson in Tehran', 'Exile and Entropy' and 'Marco Polo' were previously published in *Ashes in the Air* (UQP, 2011); 'Listening to Michael Jackson in Tehran' in *Over There: Poems from Singapore and Australia*, eds John Kinsella and Alvin Pang (Ethos Books, 2008); 'Exile and Entropy' in *Reflecting on Melbourne*, eds Janette Fernando and Jean Sietzema-Dickson (Poetica Christi Press, 2009); 'Marco Polo' in *The Best Australian Poems 2008*, ed. Peter Rose (Black Inc.) and *Heat*; 'I, the Monster' in *Divan*; 'Rumi' in *Going Down Swinging* and *The Penguin Anthology of Australian Poetry*, ed. John Kinsella (Penguin, 2008).

Louis Armand
Textbase for 'Patrick White as a Headland' and 'Utzon' from *Land Partition* (2001).

'Something Like the Weather' and 'Roland Robinson's Grendel & Death in Custody' were previously published in *Letters from Ausland* (Vagabond Press, 2011); 'Roland Robinson's Grendel & Death in Custody' in *The Age*; and 'Utzon' in *Calyx: Thirty Contemporary Australian Poets*, eds Peter Minter and Michael Brennan (Paperbark Press, 2000).

Emily Ballou
UWAP for 'The Plums', 'In the Old Library', 'Plunge' and 'She Played'
from *The Darwin Poems* (2009).

'In the Old Library' was previously published in *The Sun Herald* through
The Red Room Company.

Judith Bishop
Salt Publishing for 'It Begins Where You Stand' and 'Issuance' from
Event (2007). *Australian Book Review* for 'Openings', which won the
2011 Peter Porter Poetry Prize.

'It Begins Where You Stand' was previously published in Judith Bishop's
chapbook, *Alice Missing in Wonderland* (Picaro Press, 2008); 'Issuance' in
The New Republic.

Michael Brennan
Salt Publishing for 'Letter Home ('I've tried not to think')', 'Letter
Home ('These are strange lands')' and 'The Other' from *The Imageless
World* (2003), and also for 'Letter Home ('I find him') and 'Rebirth'
from *Unanimous Night* (2008).

Michelle Cahill
'Two Souls', 'Kissing Hamlet', 'The Stinking Mantra' and 'Night Birds'
were previously published in *Vishvarūpa* (Five Islands Press, 2011); 'Two
Souls' in *Seva Bharati Journal of English Studies*; 'Kissing Hamlet' in
Etchings; 'Night Birds' in *Australian Literary Review*.

Elizabeth Campbell
'Proverb' was previously published in *Letters to the Tremulous Hand* (John
Leonard Press, 2007); 'Fear' and 'Dalkey Island' in *Error* (John Leonard
Press, 2011).

Justin Clemens
Hunter Publishers for 'Whirl', 'Down', 'Morning' and 'Balladia
Libidinalia' from *Villain* (2009).

'Trying to Buy That What They Have Not Got' was previously published in *Me 'n' Me Trumpet* (Vagabond Press, 2011).

Joel Deane
Australian Scholarly Publishing for 'Guantanamo' and 'Man to Woman' from *Magisterium* (2008).

'Divertimento' was previously published in *Meanjin*; 'I Build a Little House Where Our Hearts Once Lived' in *Australian Book Review* and *Subterranean Radio Songs* (Interactive Press, 2005).

Kate Fagan
'Dadabase' was previously published in *Blackbox Manifold*; 'Concrete Poem' in *The Penguin Anthology of Australian Poetry*, ed. John Kinsella (Penguin, 2008); 'Letter IV: On Reality' in *The Best Australian Poems 2009*, ed. Robert Adamson (Black Inc.); 'Letter IV: On Reality' and 'Letter XI: Agape (Reprise)' from 'The Correspondence' in *Ekleksographia*. All of Kate Fagan's poems in this anthology will appear in a new collection from Giramondo Publishing.

The source texts for 'Dadabase' are Tristan Tzara et al., 'DADA Manifesto'; Tristan Tzara, 'Proclamation without Pretension' and 'Seven Dada Manifestos and Lampisteries'; Johanna Drucker, *The Visible Word*; and Michael Farrell, 'realm of humour', 'honeyimhotel', 'codas', 'sumumn', 'sprinter', 'after jim showed his bum the evening slid', 'writing 2nd ave pts 1 & 2', 'preludes', 'dream affect', 'fhue dahnn I' and 'the orange household'.

The source texts for 'A Little Song' are Gertrude Stein, *The World is Round*; and WB Yeats, 'Before the World was Made', Part I of 'Supernatural Songs', 'Chosen', 'Lullaby', 'Lapis Lazuli', Parts II and III of 'The Tower' and 'The Happy Townland'.

Jane Gibian
Giramondo Publishing for 'Continuity', 'Parts of the tongue', 'Ardent' and 'summer sequence' from *Ardent* (2007).

'Sound piece' was previously published in *The Best Australian Poems 2009*, ed. Robert Adamson (Black Inc.); 'tidemark' in *Overland*.

Lisa Gorton
Australian Book Review for 'Dreams and Artefacts', which was shortlisted for the 2010 Peter Porter Poetry Prize. Giramondo Publishing for 'The Affair' from *Press Release* (2007).

'The Humanity of Abstract Painting' was previously published in *Before and After Science: The 2010 Adelaide Biennial of Australian Art*, eds Sarah Tutton and Charlotte Day, and in *The Best Australian Poems 2010*, ed. Robert Adamson (Black Inc.). 'Mistletoe' was previously published in the catalogue to Rebecca Mayo and Marian Crawford's 2010 art exhibition, *Regeneration*, at RMIT Project Space.

Libby Hart
'In Development' and 'The Dream Jar' were previously published in *Fresh News from the Arctic* (Interactive Press, 2006). 'Lone Figure – *Malin Head*', 'Woman Drawing the Curtains of Her Bedroom – *Carrick-on-Shannon*', 'Lone Figure – *Annaghmakerrig*', 'Widower Sitting on the Edge of His Bed – *Kinsale*' and 'Woman – *Bray Head*' were previously published in *This Floating World* (Five Islands Press, 2011). 'The Dream Jar' was also previously published in *Road of Shadows*; 'Lone Figure – *Annaghmakerrig*' in *THE SHOp*; 'Lone Figure – *Malin Head*' and 'Widower Sitting on the Edge of His Bed – *Kinsale*' in *Cordite*; 'Woman – *Bray Head*' in *Island*.

Sarah Holland-Batt
'This Landscape Before Me' was previously published in *Poetry*; 'Night Sonnet' in *Blast*; 'The Art of Disappearing' and 'The Sewing Room' in *Aria* (UQP, 2008).

LK Holt
'The Children and the World' and 'Portrait with Red Bird' were previously published in *Man Wolf Man* (John Leonard Press, 2007); 'False Starts', 'Girls' and 'From Inside the MRI Scanner' in *Patience, Mutiny* (John Leonard Press, 2010).

Emma Jones
Faber & Faber for 'Tiger in the Menagerie', 'Conversation', 'Paradise', 'Painting' and 'Painted Tigers' from *The Striped World* (2009).

Danijela Kambaskovic-Sawers
'A Migrant Writer on a Bus (Thinking About Kundera)' was previously published in *Westerly*; 'The Williad (The Epic on the Epic, *Écriture Feminine*): The Writer and the Monsters of Child and Housework' in *Cordite*; 'Return to Kalevala' in *Masthead*. 'Rapunzel to the Prince 3' and 'Circe to Ulysses 5' will appear in *Internal Monologues: A Romance*, forthcoming from Fremantle Press.

Bronwyn Lea
Giramondo Publishing for 'Two Ways Out', 'The Nightgown' and 'Born Again' from *The Other Way Out* (2008).

'Antipodes' and 'The Chinese Foot' were previously published in *Flight Animals* (UQP, 2001); 'The Flood' in *Australian Literary Review*.

Cameron Lowe:
'The Sum', 'Morning Light' and 'Requested' were previously published in *Porch Music* (Whitmore Press, 2010); 'The Sum' and 'Requested' in *Cordite*.

John Mateer
Fremantle Press for 'Ode', 'Splitter Falls, Lorne', 'Those Immigrants', 'One Year' and 'The Long Man of Wilmington' from *The West* (2010).

Kate Middleton
Giramondo Publishing for 'The Queen's Ocean' and 'Colorado River Prayer' from *Fire Season* (2009).

Esther Ottaway
'Ocean Nocturne' was previously published in *The Sun Herald* through The Red Room Company; 'Liminal Love Songs' in *Heat*; 'Dimension and Light' in *Blood Universe* (Poets Union, 2006).

Claire Potter
'Eurydice's Cellar', 'A While' and 'Ladies of the Canon' were previously published in *Swallow* (Five Islands Press, 2010).

'A While' is for Robert Adamson, and reprises his poem 'Fishing in a Landscape for Love', *The Goldfinches of Baghdad* (Flood Editions, 2006).

'Ladies of the Canon' is after 'Ladies of the Canyon', an album released in 1970 by Joni Mitchell, and 'The Garden' and 'The Cycads', poems by Judith Wright, *Woman to Man* (Angus & Robertson, 1967).

David Prater
'Sunbathing' was previously published in *Overland*; 'Oz' in *Jacket*; 'Lurker' in *The Sun Herald* through The Red Room Company; 'A821.4' in *PFS Post*.

Nick Riemer
Puncher & Wattmann for 'The Bird, the Year', 'Park André Citroën in Winter' and 'The Meaning Plain: 40 Aerial Shots' from *James Stinks (and so does Chuck)* (2006). *Australian Book Review* for 'The Thing You're In'.

Jaya Savige
'Summer Fig', 'Dransfield in Bavaria', 'The Pain Switch' and 'La Quercia del Tasso' were previously published in *Surface to Air* (UQP, 2011); 'Summer Fig' in *The Best Australian Poems 2010*, ed. Robert Adamson (Black Inc.) and *The Weekend Australian*; 'The Pain Switch' in *The Best Australian Poems 2010*, ed. Robert Adamson (Black Inc.) and *The Age*; 'La Quercia del Tasso' in *Heat*.

Maria Takolander
Salt Publishing for 'Tableaux' and 'Canasta for Lovers' from *Ghostly Subjects* (2010).

'Anaesthetic' was previously published in *The Best Australian Poems 2010*, ed. Robert Adamson (Black Inc.) and *Island*; 'Unborn' in *Meanjin*; '47 Degrees' in *Westerly*.

Samuel Wagan Watson

'Floodlight Sonatas', 'Jetty Nights', 'Bone Yard, South Brisbane', 'Revolver' and 'Night Racing' were previously published in *Smoke Encrypted Whispers* (UQP, 2004).

Simon West

Puncher & Wattmann for '*Marnpi Rockhole* by Mick Namarara Tjapaltjarri' from *First Names* (2006).

Petra White

'Magnolia Tree' was previously published in *The Age*; 'Karri Forest' in *The Incoming Tide* (John Leonard Press, 2007); 'Notes for the Time Being' and 'The Gone' in *The Simplified World* (John Leonard Press, 2010).